THE TREE OF DEATH, AND OTHER HILARIOUS STORIES

ALSO BY MARC SCHMATJEN

My Giraffe Makes Me Laugh – A rhyming picture book

The Sycamore Detective Agency – Children's fiction - Action/adventure/detective/mystery

THE TREE OF DEATH, AND OTHER HILARIOUS STORIES

The *Just a Smidge* Anthology - Volume I

www.justasmidge.com

To the Roland Family — Keep Laughing! — Marc

MARC SCHMATJEN

For my beautiful wife, Sandy, who has inexplicably put up with this for all these years

CONTENTS

Preface

The Name
June 22, 2008

I am a fourth-generation American who was born and raised in California, but you would never guess that when looking at my name, so I really feel like I should start with an explanation. It's spelled Schmatjen. It's pronounced "Smidgen", like a smidgen of this, and a smidgen of that. No one in the family knows why. It's German, but some kind of strange hill-people German that were more Austrian, or more Swiss, or more drunk than regular Germans.

So we all went by "Smidge." Once you pronounce it for people, that's your nickname. No getting around it, and all in all it's a pretty good deal for a kid. There is never really any doubt about what you might get called later in life. If you're destined for a certain nickname, it's nice to know ahead of time that it's going to be palatable. No chewing your nails wondering what fate might befall you on the playground. Through a twist of fate will I forever be branded "Stinky" or "Monkey Butt?" Nope. Not with a last name like Schmatjen.

In the Schmatjen clan, there is a general rule that because of the last name's inherent spelling and pronunciation issues, the first names had better be fool-proof. So, inexplicably, my folks named me Marc with a "C." I'm not sure what they were thinking at the time, but looking back on it, it seems ill-advised. I have always liked it, but it invariably adds an extra dimension to the name explaining process that we Schmatjens constantly go through. I have learned from this experience, and have named all three of my boys very common and traditionally-spelled names. Constantinople, Madagascar & Lyb'ya are the apples of my eye!

One upside to having Schmatjen as a last name is that any other Schmatjen you catch wind of is one hundred percent, definitely related to you. Take that, Smith and Johnson! I am proud to have three sons that will someday perpetuate the Schmatjen name. Not because I am overly fond of it, but more because having more Schmatjens out in the world increases the chance, however minutely, that one of us will become famous enough that the rest of us can stop having to explain how to pronounce and spell the damn name!

1

Life in General

Life is funny - Marc. My words.

Soap
February 2, 2011

My wife has been couponing. This is a new sport for shoppers involving laying out thousands of dollars on ranch dressing and ketchup, because the price was so low, "it was practically free," and then giving them away to friends and family because you ended up with five hundred bottles of each. She swears to me that we are saving money by stocking up on things we don't need, but I remain skeptical.

One item in particular became a point of contention recently. She came home with six big squeeze bottles of "Men's Hair and Body Wash." I asked her why in the world she had bought me liquid body wash, to which she answered the typical coupon addict's response of, "It was so cheap, they were practically giving it away."

My main problem with that recurring answer is that there is a certain amount of money between "actually" and "practically" when it comes to giving things away at the store.

She then told me that she planned to stop buying bar soap for the shower. I was to immediately begin washing myself with liquid "Energy Wash" that would "Recharge and Energize without Drying" (With mint extracts!). I politely explained that that was not going to happen, and she should return the bushel of body wash to the store. She calmly informed me about the coupon return policy restrictions, and politely inquired as to why I was such a stubborn jackass. I told her that my bar soap worked just fine, and then went on to state my case about how I don't think we're actually saving money when she buys things we don't need, just because they are on sale. She didn't see it my way.

After a few days and approximately three hundred requests from my wife for me to "try the damn body wash," I gave in.

One of my main objections to using body wash was that I didn't want to have to use her weird looking, pink, loofa-like, spongy, spidery, half-sandpaper/half-shammy-cloth thing-a-ma-jig that hangs on a rope from our shower handle. It looks like someone tied a pink fishnet into a knot the size of a grapefruit, and the only thing it does is collect shockingly cold water and dead skin cells. Besides being disgusting, it's a tool that I just don't want to have to use.

I like bar soap. Bar soap is ingenious. You pick it up and use it, and when it disappears you know it's time for a new one. It is self-cleaning, and there are no appurtenances, tools, holders, delivery containers, devices, or spongy loofa things. It's just you and the soap. Simple.

She listened calmly to my hesitations about using her squishy pink bacteria farm-on-a-rope, then she rolled her eyes and explained - in the same voice she uses when she is helping one of our children figure out a ridiculously simple problem - that I obviously did not need to use her bath sponge. I could just squirt the body wash into my hand, and proceed to soap myself up. Since the body wash was apparently un-returnable, I gave in and told her I would give it a try. She thanked me profusely in the same voice she uses to thank police officers for speeding tickets.

The next morning, it was go time. I hopped into the shower, strangely enthusiastic about my new cleansing adventure. Maybe I would love the body wash. Maybe I would discover a whole new world of instant morning refreshment. It was, after all, "energy" wash that promised to "recharge and energize" me through the deft and patented use of non-drying mint extracts.

Here's how my body wash experience went:
1) Grabbed bottle of energizing body wash from shower caddy.
2) Unscrewed the large blue bottle top on the squeeze bottle and stared down into the 3/4-inch-diameter opening.
3) Thought to myself, "How does this work? This stuff is going to come out of here fast."
4) Smelled the energy wash. Mmmm. Minty.
5) Further pondered the large opening.
6) Examined the large blue bottle top in my other hand and finally noticed the flip-top cap on top.
7) Screwed large blue bottle top back onto bottle and flipped flip-top open.
8) Looked at much, much smaller squeeze-bottle delivery hole and decided that was the way to go.
9) Squeezed large handful of bright-blue minty energy wash into my right hand.
10) Flipped flip-top closed and set bottle of energy wash back in shower caddy.
11) Washed top of left forearm.
12) Ran out of minty energy wash.
13) Retrieved bottle of energy wash from shower caddy.
14) Flipped open flip-top lid.
15) Squeezed even larger handful of bright-blue minty energy wash into right hand.
16) Flipped flip-top closed and set bottle of energy wash back in shower caddy.

17) Washed bottom of left forearm and elbow.
18) Ran out of minty energy wash.
19) Did some quick math in my head.
20) Decided that if I needed to keep opening the bottle and getting more minty energy wash every three seconds, I would be two and a half hours late to work.
21) Left minty energy body wash in shower caddy.
22) Picked up bar of soap.
23) Washed my body.
24) Put soap back in soap tray.
25) Turned off water.
26) Toweled off.
27) Threw bottle of super-minty energy-style hair and body wash into trash can.

I informed my wife that the experiment had failed, and as a side note, that it did nothing to energize me at all, mint extracts or not.

She informed me that I was a Neanderthal and just simply did not know how to use body wash properly.

I'm a pretty smart guy. What am I missing, here? How is body wash supposed to be even remotely as convenient or useful as bar soap? I asked my wife that question, which she refused to answer. She just mumbled something about how cheap it was. I guess in the couponer's mind, price goes a long way toward necessity and usefulness.

As far as the "recharge and energize" claim, I still haven't figured that one out. Maybe it's caffeinated and I was really supposed to drink it.

El Arbol de Muerte
March 30, 2011

Our house came with six fairly good-sized trees. Two in the front yard and four in the back. It occurred to me the other day that I know absolutely nothing about them. I have no idea what kind they are. I know one of the two in the front yard is some kind of pine tree and all the others are the kinds that lose their leaves. That's all I've got.

We'll get to the reason why it occurred to me that I didn't know anything about them in a minute. When I realized my lack of knowledge on the tree subject, I also realized that they are the only things I own that I don't know a single thing about. I can't think of anything else that I own that I am so wholesale ignorant about as my foliage. They just came with the house.

I could tell you at least seven details about my fence right off the top of my head. I know lots of really un-interesting facts about the water heater. I know the tonnage of my air conditioner, and the BTU rating of my furnace. I know what the roof is made of, the R-value of my insulation, and all about the inner workings of the toilets. Those things all came with the house, just like the trees did, but for some reason, I have no knowledge, nor do I have any interest in gaining any knowledge, about the trees.

Actually, it's not just the trees, but the bushes as well. I couldn't be less interested in them. When we bought the house a few years back, one of the first things I did was figure out the automatic watering system. There are in-ground sprinklers for both lawns, and a drip-line system that runs around the entire outer edge of the property, servicing all the trees and shrubbery. The first thing I did was turn off the drip system.

I simply do not feel the need to spend my time and money maintaining a drip line system and buying water for flora that should be able to survive just fine without my help. Plenty of trees and shrubs out there survive on just the water God sees fit to give them, and I don't think mine should have any kind of special treatment above and beyond that. I don't want to coddle them! I figure, if they survive, great. If they don't, then it wasn't meant to be.

Truth be told, I really only water the grass because it's not socially acceptable to let it go native, either. I really don't like spending my money hydrating something that grows perfectly fine on its own, just because my neighbors and my wife think it should be green year-round and be mowed every week during the summer. But, in this life, you must pick your battles.

As you may have guessed, I don't exactly have a "green thumb." I don't know if my inability to care about plant species identification and welfare stems from my lack of ability to cultivate them, or vice-versa, but either way, it's just not there. That became abundantly clear to me last year when our garden failed miserably.

Now, don't misunderstand. I do water the garden. I have no problem with that, because the garden usually pays me back with produce. Our past gardens had done OK, producing what I considered a healthy amount of tomatoes, zucchini, and the occasional jalapeño pepper. Last year, however, we grew exactly one strawberry, four tomatoes, and zero zucchini. Most of the plants themselves grew a little, but produced basically no fruit at all. If you have ever grown zucchini, then you know its plant is like a weed. Normally, you have to be careful how close you plant them to everything else, because they will grow at a rate of three feet per hour and take over the whole garden. Last year they got about eight inches tall and quit. How could that have gone wrong?

I was lamenting our garden's plight to a friend at a late-summer dinner party last year, and she began giving me some pretty startling facts.

"Did the zucchini plants ever flower?"
"Yes, but then, no zucchinis grew and the flowers just withered and fell off."
"OK, well you would have had male flowers and female flowers. The flowers just never pollenated each other. You probably didn't have enough bees."
"I don't have any bees that I know of. Am I supposed to have some?"
"Well, if you don't have enough bees, you need to pollenate the female flowers by hand."
"Excuse me?"

This was news to me. I have to do stuff? I thought these things just took care of themselves, like my trees and bushes. And I'm not sure I want to pollenate by hand. The zucchini plants and I have a professional relationship, and getting involved in any kind of pollination activities seems much too personal. I think I'll just go to the store instead.

Anyway… back to the trees. The thing that got me thinking about how little I really know about my trees was something Son Number One said the other day. One of the trees in our front yard (the one that loses its leaves) turns bright white at the beginning of spring. It sprouts a million tiny white flowers that make for a really nice looking tree for a few weeks, but there is one problem. They smell like death.

These beautiful little flowers give off the unmistakable aroma of rotting flesh. That whiff you get when you walk out into the garage and your brain says, "Dead rat." That's what the tree smells like. We have a lot of them in my neighborhood, so for the first few weeks of spring, our street is really pretty, but really stinky.

Number One and I were on the way to kindergarten the other morning, and he pipes up from the back seat, "Hey Daddy. Look at how many death trees there are around here!"

My son was just repeating what he had heard me call the trees, but it got me thinking. Maybe I should learn their real name before we get a call from a concerned teacher.

"Why is your son talking about a 'death tree' in his front yard? Is there something you need to tell us, sir?"

On the other hand, the real name, whatever it may be, won't tell the story even half as well as, "Death Tree." If that isn't their real name, it should be. The plant nurseries might disagree with me, however. Something tells me sales of "death trees" might lag a little behind Japanese elms. Maybe they could use the Spanish name.

"El Arbol de Muerte" has a nice ring to it. Come to think of it, I'm going to start telling the boys that's the name of the tree. They won't know the difference, and they'll sound a lot smarter!

Ignorance is bliss, as long as you don't sound stupid, right?

The Mama Bear
June 22, 2011

We went camping with friends this past weekend at Sugar Pine Point State Park at Lake Tahoe. We were expecting a fun weekend of campfires, hiking, and swimming, but we ended up getting much more than we bargained for. By the time the weekend was through, our kids had some great bear stories and I had a brand new wife.

We arrived Friday afternoon and listened to a ten-minute bear advisory lecture from the park ranger, complete with an affidavit we were required to sign, stating that we understood the bear rules and would gladly be subject to a $1000 fine if we did not keep our food and toiletries locked in the big, green, steel bear lockers provided at the campsites.

OK, OK, we get it. There are bears here. We'll put the food away. Can we go to our campsites now?

We set up camp in two adjoining campsites and had a fun evening of men setting up tents and making fires, women laughing at the men's lack of skill in the tent and fire-making departments, and little boys playing in the woods and peeing on trees. Dinner and s'mores and off to bed without a bear in sight. Good times.

I had a book signing back in our home town the next day, so I got up early and drove the two hours back to our house to take a shower. I went off to the bookstore and occasionally received a text message from my wife about something or other to bring back with me that afternoon. When my phone rang around two o'clock, I was expecting to hear about another camping-related item that we'd left behind. Not so.

What I heard my wife say was, "We've had some bears. They're stalking our campsite."

Hmmm. That's different than what I thought you were going to say, honey. As the ever-concerned father figure, my first question was, "Is everyone OK?"

After she assured me that everyone was safe and in good spirits I switched to ever-financially-vigilant breadwinner mode. "Is the State Parks Service going to fine us $1000?"

Luckily, the answer to the first question was yes and the second question was no. She then had to hang up because the park rangers had just arrived at our campsite for the second time that afternoon to get the latest bear report. I drove really fast back to the lake.

When I arrived back at the campsite an hour and a half later, the rangers were still there. "Have they been here the whole time?" I asked.

"No, we just had a third bear about ten minutes ago," my wife answered casually, as if close bear encounters were a common occurrence in her life. "I tracked him through the woods until they got here."

Excuse me? You did what? I have been away for nine and a half hours and when I get back you are tracking bears? What in the hell happened while I was gone?

Here's the condensed version my wife and our friends, Jeff and Carrie, told me:

They woke up shortly after I had left, had a leisurely breakfast, went on a long hike, and came back to camp and made lunch. They were all assembled together eating at the picnic table in Jeff and Carrie's campsite, but my wife had left one of our plastic storage bins out of the bear locker and on top of the table

10

in our campsite. No one thought anything of it, since they were close by, until Jeff saw the bear coming through the woods. They watched in awe as the 300-pound black bear walked into our campsite, a mere 25 yards away, and knocked the bin off the table. He (or she) grabbed our big bag of marshmallows and sat down for a delicious and delightfully fluffy snack.

By this time, three adults and five boys had been shoehorned into Jeff and Carrie's midsize SUV, and were driving away from the bear toward the ranger station. While they were busy alerting the ranger to their predicament, the bear devoured our entire box of graham crackers.

The rangers came back to the campsite with them and shooed the bear away by yelling at it and banging pots and pans together. When the bear had retreated, the rangers explained the "no food left out farther away than arm's reach" rule which we had missed during bear orientation the day before. It was at this point that my wife asked the rangers, while crying, if the bear would come back. They reassuringly said, "No."

Apparently the rangers don't speak for the bears. They obviously did not take into account the fact that the bear had unfinished business, because he came back about a half-hour later looking for the crucial third and final ingredient to his lunch of s'mores. To the bruin's dismay, the chocolate bars were locked up tight, and he was out of luck.

Over the initial shock of their close proximity to long-clawed wildlife, Jeff and my wife shooed him away on their own this time while Carrie took the five boys for a nice ride back to the ranger station. Knowing my wife, I think at this point she had gone from being scared to being aggravated that this thing was threatening the safety of her children, not to mention putting a severe damper on the night's dessert.

When the rangers arrived back at our campsite, they questioned my wife on which way the bear had gone after she and Jeff had shooed it away. Unbeknownst to the rangers, by involving my wife in the hunt for the bear, they had apparently deputized her as an assistant park ranger in her own mind. This became shockingly obvious to everyone a few hours later when a new bear showed up near our campsite. Upon spotting the interloping omnivore, my wife casually asked Jeff and Carrie if they would keep an eye on the boys while she went off and made sure this pesky varmint didn't cause any trouble around these here parts.

Into the woods she went, armed with the formidable defensive weapons of choice, the universally-feared pot and pan combo. She quietly stalked the bear through the underbrush, making sure she could relay the beast's exact coordinates to her new comrades-in-arms when they arrived. I guess her plan was to fall back on her extensive deputy park ranger training by banging the pot and pan together if the bear showed any signs of annoyance at being followed.

Thankfully, the actual rangers with actual guns showed up and took over before she was forced to make a move with her deadly cookware. What a difference a few bear sightings can make! My wife went from suburban housewife to Grizzly Adams in the span of two hours. I am convinced that if a fourth bear had showed up before I had arrived, she surely would have slipped off her shoes, clamped a kitchen knife between her teeth, and tried to sneak up on it from behind to teach it a lesson about messing with her kids and her meal plans.

The really funny part is, if I had been there and even hinted at wanting to shoo the bear off, either by myself, or with Jeff by my side, she would have asked in an exasperated and slightly panicked voice, "Are you crazy? Do you want your boys to grow up without a father?"

It just goes to show you, there's no telling what a mama bear is going to do.

Soap, Part II
September 14, 2011

Our boys have started to take showers on their own. Up until now, we had been giving them baths. The decision to move to the shower was spurred mostly by the fact that all three of them don't fit in the bathtub together anymore, and giving three individual baths really cuts into my TV time.

I still have to give Son Number Three baths, but it was about time the older two started pulling their own weight in the personal hygiene department. Plus, we really wanted to see if the shower in their bathroom actually worked. We have lived in our current house for almost three years now, and up until this week, no one had ever used it. When I finally got the handle to turn, after the loud clanging noise subsided, water actually came out of the showerhead, so we were good to go.

After the Body Wash Incident of Early 2011, my wife has been sure to keep me stocked with plenty of good old-fashioned bar soap. Since my wife has inexplicably stuck with the body wash, and the kids' baths get done with baby shampoo, up until now, our bar soap had been used only by me. So, this week was Son Number One and Two's first experience trying to wash themselves with a big bar of soap. Witnessing that slippery learning curve instantly flooded me with childhood memories of soap. I had a strange upbringing, soap-wise.

My dad was a pilot for Delta Airlines. In the early days of his career, with a wife at home raising three small kids, he would always bring the little bars of unopened hotel soap and the small bottles of shampoo home from his trips to help with the household budget. His flight schedule usually had him gone multiple days at a time, so he collected a lot of soap. So much so, that we never ran out. As the years went by, the Hilton/Marriott/Ramada soap harvesting never stopped. I

13

showered with a tiny, fits-in-the-palm-of-your-hand bar of soap from my very first shower until I was eighteen years old. (Actually, I showered with a different one every other day. They don't last very long.) As a result, I never had any early childhood regular-sized soap training.

I vividly remember the first time I used a real bar of soap. I was at least six or seven years old, and we were staying with my grandparents while my parents went on a week's vacation. I stepped into the unfamiliar shower and was immediately transfixed by the GIGANTIC bar of BRIGHT GREEN soap. (The hotel soap was always either white, tan, or the occasional exciting off-pink.) This was Irish Spring, and it smelled AMAZING. (The hotel soap smelled like almonds, talc, or nothing.) This giant, magical, colorful, brick-sized bar of cleanliness filled the entire shower with some heavenly, yet previously unknown fragrance. Apparently - based on the TV commercials of the 1970s - it was supposed to remind me of the wonderful smell of a lush green Irish glade near a waterfall where I was walking hand-in-hand with a bonny lass in a turtleneck sweater, but since I had never done that, I didn't recognize the smell. To me it just smelled strong and wonderfully different.

Then I tried to pick it up and use it. Now, big bars of soap are hard to handle for any six-year-old, but to a lad that had previously only worked with soap the size of a bite-size candy bar, this slimy behemoth was almost totally unmanageable. I must have dropped it, picked it up, and dropped it again a hundred times. The racket coming from the shower got so loud that my grandma came in to check on me, but I was so embarrassed about not being able to work the soap, I told her that everything was just fine, and that I obviously didn't need any help. She left unconvinced.

After a half-hour of soap hockey, I finally ended up attempting to soap myself up while holding onto the massive slippery green bar with two hands at once. That is a pretty difficult maneuver,

14

and I'm not sure how clean I actually got myself that day. Marginal hygienic success aside, it was one of the most memorable days of my childhood, so taken was I by the giant, fragrant green soap.

If asked to come up with the defining TV characters of their childhood, most guys my age would probably list the likes of Superman, The Fonz, Mean Joe Green, Bo and Luke Duke, etc.

I'm guessing very few would list an actor from a soap commercial. To my list, however, I must include the guy in the snappy turtleneck and sport coat, standing in the field, cutting the bar of Irish Spring open with his pocket knife. When I saw that commercial as a kid, I thought to myself, "Yeah, I was that guy for a day. Fresh and (insert wolf-whistle here), clean as a whistle!"

But alas, that one shower was the extent of my Irish Spring glory as a child. My parents came back from vacation, and it was small soap business as usual again.

There was, however, one major up-side to growing up with miniature soap. As kids, we never had our mouths "washed out with soap," a la Ralphie in *A Christmas Story*, sitting with the bar of Lifebuoy in his mouth. My mom was probably afraid we'd accidentally swallow the hotel soap.

My boys won't be so lucky. I've got plenty of full-size bars of Irish Spring. I love that stuff!

2

<u>The Holidays</u>

Nothing is more magical than holidays with children. Nothing is more strange, more unpredictable, more expensive, or more mentally taxing than holidays with children, either.

<u>Dear Santa</u>
December 23, 2008

Dear Santa,

All I want for Christmas is a LoJack for Snot Rod. Oh, and one for a baby spoon. Allow me to explain.

Last Christmas you brought my sons some Matchbox-type toy cars from the Disney movie *Cars*. One of them was the orange GTO with the big racing slicks, the supercharger, and the cylinder head-cold, named "Snot Rod." My four-year-old has grown quite attached to it over the last few months and likes to take it everywhere now. Likewise, my two-year-old has developed a fondness for carrying around spoons. He likes measuring spoons, wooden spoons, silverware, and most of all, baby spoons. He has a particular type that is his favorite. The "pokey baby spoony" as he calls it. It's a metal spoon with a big, fat, plastic handle. We used to have a lot of them, but now we only have one. That's because of the problem.

My boys really have no short-term memory at all. That's the problem. They cherish a certain item almost more than life itself, but cannot remember where they set it down thirty seconds ago. Now, since Snot Rod and the baby spoon are both less than four inches in length and our house is thirty-four hundred square feet not counting the garage, you can see my dilemma.

Our boys aren't allowed to take toys to bed, so they request that they be allowed to leave certain toys right outside their door for when they wake up. Occasionally (read: All the time) they get their heart set on a toy that they have recently misplaced. When this happens, it is important to gauge the level of heart-setted-ness. If it is high, you have two choices. Find the toy and put it outside their door so they will be happy in the morning, and hopefully entertained, or don't find it, don't leave it outside their door, and hear about that decision at 5:45 A.M.

Tonight was a night with a high heart-set-titude rating for Snot Rod. My wife and I were lucky enough to be able to go out to a movie this evening by ourselves since Grandma and Grandpa are here awaiting your arrival tomorrow night. When we got back, well past both of our bed times, I was obliged to look for Snot Rod. The last sighting had been in the car. Oh joy. Well, off to the garage I went, flashlight in hand, to contort myself onto the floor mats to be able to inspect under the seats as well as between the car seats in kid row.

Here's an abbreviated list of what I found:
Six Cheerios
Twelve raisins
One bell
Five Matchbox cars (one of them was orange, but it wasn't Snot Rod)
Two Dr. Seuss books
One Thomas Guide of Sacramento
Two baby wipes (unused, thank the Lord)
Seven acorns

One pinecone
Thirty-two goldfish crackers
Six pretzels
Three Legos
One sock

Here's a list of what I did not find:
Snot Rod

After resigning myself to the fact that I would be dealing with a disappointed child in the pre-dawn hours, I went upstairs to sit down at my desk. I worked at my computer for thirty minutes before I glanced to my left. And can you guess what was sitting right on top of my desk, not fourteen inches away from my left hand? Snot Rod.

So what I would really like for Christmas this year is a few small tracking devices that I can attach to the toy-du-jour. I really think a lot of time and sanity could be saved if your elves could come up with something compact that has a strong signal. We could also use a few for the sippy cups, and the binkies. Also, with regard to my wife, one for the TV remote, the cordless phone, her keys, and her cell phone. And one for Grandma's cell phone. And her keys. On second thought, why don't you just bring me a whole bunch of them and I'll take it from there. It wouldn't be a bad idea to just LoJack the boys themselves when we head for the park or the mall!

I guess maybe I'd like some sort of desk organizer, too.

Thanks Santa!

The Five Feet of Christmas I Despise
December 2, 2009

Since I'm a Christian, I really enjoy Christmas. We get to celebrate the birth of Jesus Christ with our family and friends, joyfully thanking God for His greatest gift to us. And besides, I really love sugar cookies! There is, however, one aspect of Christmas that I don't like. Actually, "don't like" isn't strong enough. Loath. Hate. Despise… yes, there is one aspect of Christmas that I despise. It has to do with Christmas lights.

It's not the lights themselves. I love those. I really like the way they make the house look. My wife likes icicle lights; the kind with the individual light strands of differing lengths that hang down from the eaves to simulate a sparkling frozen wonderland. They give the house a warm glow while at the same time making us feel like we have a winter paradise in our otherwise non-frozen California front yard. It's really quite magical, and brings joy to my heart every time I pull into the driveway from work.

It's not putting up the lights, either. I don't mind that chore. I might even go so far as to say that I enjoy it. It's usually a nice, crisp fall day. I'm bundled up against the early December breeze, high on a ladder, as the boys frolic in the red and yellow autumn leaves on the lawn below. They "help" by holding the ladder, and climbing up to my feet when I'm down low. It seems like the essence of being a father and a family man is all wrapped up in that one chore, and it makes me feel content with my life.

The problem comes when I plug them in. Night falls, and I make the extension cord connection and then stand back to proudly admire my work. And there it is. The five feet of Christmas I despise: The five-foot section of icicle lights that is out, right in the middle of the string.

Dark. Nada.

We've got plug end, five feet of lit string, five feet of dark string, five more feet of lit string, and the prong end. Awesome! Right in the middle of the front of the house. My house could be a magical, sparkling, winter wonderland, but instead, that five-foot section of lights, out of the ninety-five total feet of lights, makes the entire house look stupid. The five-foot outage actually takes the whole effort and turns it upside down. Instead of improving the look of the house for the holidays, I have detracted from it, and made it look like the Christmas equivalent of the neighborhood delinquent's house where the lawn is never mowed, there's a car with a two-inch layer of dirt and four flat tires in the driveway, and the screen door is hanging on one hinge. What a wonderful night!

My wife comes out and asks, "Didn't you check them before you put them up?"
I grit my teeth.

My smart-ass neighbor yells from across the street, "You missed a spot!"
Yeah, thanks, Ted. Why don't you go back inside now?

My son asks, "How come you didn't put any lights right there?"
Time for you to go inside now, too, junior.

I would fix it, but I don't know how. I don't understand how it's possible. Is the electricity jumping from one spot to another in the cord, bypassing some of the lights? How on Earth can both ends of a continuous string of lights be lit, but the middle is dark? It's like turning the hose on at the house, cutting it in half in the middle, and still getting water out the other end.

I'm almost positive I used that string last year and it worked, otherwise I wouldn't have kept it for this year, right? So please tell me what happened to it while it was tucked away in a plastic

20

tub in my garage for the past eleven months. Did the copper wires melt during the summer? Did the electrons go on vacation? Does it just hate me?

To make troubleshooting even harder, I can't recreate the problem on a string that works. I'm fairly sure it isn't a bad bulb, because I can pull the tiny individual bulbs out of their tiny two-copper-wire-prong sockets in the lit strings, and the rest of the string stays lit. Why? Can someone please tell me why? Please! Why???

Oh, well. At least the Christmas tree lights work. Wait a minute.... The whole left side just went out. Great! Someone find the lawnmower while I fix this screen door hinge.

I need a sugar cookie.

Santa Overload
December 22, 2009

Halloween was a month-long event this year. Between school parties, play dates, moms club parties and the actual night, I think my kids dressed up in their costumes every other day for the entire month of October. I thought that was a little excessive.

Then it was a quick transition to hand-print turkeys and construction paper pilgrim hats, we scarfed down some stuffing, and we were on to Christmas. If you had gone to the mall in early November, however, you would have thought that Thanksgiving was long over. There was Santa, the day after Halloween.

That's nothing compared to our home improvement warehouses, though. I kid you not, they had the Christmas stuff out at our Home Depot in September. September, people! Now, that's excessive.

It's not so much the commercialization of Christmas that I'm worried about. I actually kind of like the fact that businesses try to drag out Christmas as long as possible. It ultimately serves to give more exposure to my favorite Christian holiday, hopefully giving more people a chance to learn or remember what Christmas is really all about.

And since I was blessed with a complete lack of sympathy toward whining children, I can easily dodge the "your parents will buy you this toy for Christmas if they love you" advertising onslaught by simply telling them, "No, you can't have one of those. We're not the Rockefellers."
"What's a Rocker-Fella, Dad?"
"Zip it, kid. Get in the car."

What I *am* worried about is the amazing over-abundance of Santa sightings these days. I don't know about you, but when I was a kid, we saw Santa maybe once before Christmas if we were lucky. And that was only if we could convince our folks to take us to the mall, which was the only place you could find him.

I did a count, and my kids saw Santa no less than thirteen times this year, and actually sat on his lap at least five times. Five times! I don't think I sat on Santa's lap five times total in my entire childhood. Most years we had to write him a letter, because we could never find him to talk to him in person.

Now, the mind of a five-year-old is not as perceptive as an adult's, perhaps, but they do pick up on more than you think they will. This can be an issue, because as with any commodity, when you start flooding the system with Santas, you're going to get wide swings in the quality department.

At Son Number Two's preschool Christmas party, we had the Santa by which all others shall be judged. His beard and hair were real, he was the spitting image of old Saint Nick, his voice was perfect, he had real black boots, and his outfit was real hand-made satin and fur that puts anything else I've seen to shame. Pair him against the eighteen-year-old Santa that came to our house in the red felt and white acrylic "fur" suit. The entire suit, hat, fake beard and hair appeared as if they were made from the same materials as one of those ultra-thin, bright-red Christmas stockings that come in a six-pack from the dollar store. He had the black vinyl "booties" with the elastic strap that covered only the top half of his tennis shoes, and he was apparently too young to attempt to muster a Santa voice, so he just went with his own eighteen-year-old voice, complete with phrases like "little dude," "oh, man," and "super cool." As it turned out, however, Number Three, who is one and a half, was OK with surfer-dude Santa, but scared to death of the real deal. Go figure.

The wide variety of realism with the Santas in our encounters has left me fielding more than a few questions, like, "How come Santa's beard doesn't look the same as yesterday?" and, "Why does Santa smell like Grandpa's adult drink?"

Other questions arose this year when we ran into a proximity and time puzzle. When I took the boys to the mall to shop for Mommy, we spent a few minutes on level two peering over the railing at Santa, below in his chair, in Westfield's version of Santa wonderland, diligently taking orders from all the little boys and girls who have parents willing to wait in the Santa line at the mall. Then, off we went toward the Sears tool department, where we shop for Mommy. Along the way, not thirty seconds after we left Santa in his chair, there he was again at the portrait studio on level two. Come on, fellas! Work with me, here. At least spread out a little!

"Daddy, why is Santa right there?"
Hmmm. "So that boys and girls can get their pictures taken with him."
Crunch, crunch (sound of five-year-old's brain working overtime)
"But, he was just down there."
"Yup."
"How come?"
Hmmm. "Well, he's magic, of course. He can be in two places at once. How do you think he delivers presents to every boy and girl in the world on one night? Oh look boys, a ten-inch compound miter chop saw with a laser cut line! I'll bet Mommy would love that!"

The thing I'm most concerned about is not the questions, and it's not the daunting requirement for spontaneous yet non-conflicting answers. It's the loss of wonder that I want to avoid. The boys will only be young for a short period of time, and I want them to be mystified by Santa for as long as possible, not bored with him.

This year we have seen Santa five times at the mall, five times at Christmas parties, once on the Polar Express, and once on a fire truck in our neighborhood. Oh, yeah, and once driving a Hyundai. That one was hard for my wife to explain.

Next year we'll do our best to whittle that number down a little, because I never want to hear, "Oh, look over there. It's Santa again. Ho-hum. Boring!" At least not until they're fifteen.

The Do-it-Yourself Christmas Letter
December 15, 2010

Since it is getting dangerously close to Christmas, I thought I would help you out if you have not written your Christmas letter yet. Let's face it; time is no longer on your side. There is no way you'll get anything meaningful written and out to your loved ones in time for Christmas now. Any other year, you'd be up a creek. But this year, ol' Smidgey Claus has got your back. Please feel free to use this handy do-it-yourself template to create a quality Christmas letter in nothing flat. Just fill in your last name(s) in the blanks and circle the appropriate choices, and you're in business.

Christmas 2010

Merry Christmas everyone,

We here at the _____ house have had another (great/disappointing) year. Recently, Dad received a (promotion/severe reprimand) at work, and he is still on (cloud nine/thin ice). Earlier in the year he took up (golf/drinking) and is getting really good at it. He still spends quite a bit of his free time (volunteering/womanizing) at the local (homeless shelter/homeless shelter), and has proclaimed that this year has easily been the most (rewarding/depressing) of his life.

Mom threw out her (glasses and contacts/hip) this year after getting (laser eye surgery/drunk and falling) and has been (pleased with the results/grouchy) ever since. She continues her part-time (volunteering/mandated community service) in the city and added (teaching illiterate adults to read/another 120 hours) to her (activities/sentence) when she (heard about the program from a friend/mouthed off to the judge). With all of her (giving/griping), she still finds time to (feed us/yell at us) and

26

keep us (warm and happy/guessing). She is a real (angel/piece of work).

Sister (graduated high school/stole a car) in June and was accepted into the (university/penitentiary system) in September. She has been doing (well/poorly) in her (classes/anger management therapy sessions). She has received (a nomination/little hope) from (her teachers/the warden) for (the dean's list/early release). She is now (playing tennis/appealing her case) at the (collegiate level/appellate level) and has been (in the top five/shot down by the judges) repeatedly. We couldn't be more (proud of/disappointed in) her.

Little Brother joined (the army/a cult) in the spring and completed his (basic training/new employee day) at (Fort Benning/KFC). He has been stationed (overseas/at the mall) and is on the fast track for (promotion/nothing). His (commanding officer/sixteen-year-old boss) is (pleased/apathetic) about his (natural initiative/lack of initiative), and he has received several citations for (meritorious service/marijuana possession). We are hoping he gets a transfer (back to Fort Benning/to the Mumbai KFC) so we can see (more/less) of him. We can't wait to see him (again/leave).

As for me, I finally realized my dream and got the (Ferrari 599 GTO/X-Box 360) this year. I was in (Heaven/the living room) every day this summer as I (raced professionally/ate my way) through (the streets of Milan/numerous bags of Cheetos). My (Italian girlfriend Sonia/gaming buddy Lance) recently accepted my (proposal/challenge) for (marriage/a Halo rematch), and we are going to be (married/completely useless and pale) by this time next year. I am truly living the life I've always (dreamed/been warned) about.

Well, that's about it for the latest news on the _____ family. Please (come see us/stay away) whenever you're in town. As we count our numerous (blessings/glasses of 100-

proof eggnog), we hope this letter finds you feeling as (blessed/drunk) as we feel this holiday season.

Merry Christmas!

You're welcome! Now just sign, copy and send. You're all set.

The Post-Easter Egg Hunt
April 27, 2011

We learned a few things this year when we had our annual Easter egg hunt. We do a traditional event with a few real hardboiled eggs that the kids color the day before, and a lot of snap-together brightly colored hollow plastic eggs filled with jelly beans, M&M's, and miniature candy bars. The eggs are hidden by the Easter Bunny, and the kids go haywire trying to procure as much sugar as possible in a limited timeframe.

The first thing we realized was our kids are surprisingly bad at finding small semi-hidden things. I always figured they would be really good at it, since they are closer to the ground. Not so. Most of the time, we had to stand over the egg, pointing to it, because verbal directions were just not cutting it. "It's the only bright pink thing in that otherwise completely green and brown bush! Come on, dude! How hard is that? I can see it from all the way across the lawn!"

Maybe they're all colorblind? That would explain a lot of the shirt/shorts/socks combinations that Son Number Two comes up with. My wife thinks their lack of ability to find things stems from the fact that they share my DNA. Many times she has accused me of going completely blind as soon as I open the door to the refrigerator or the pantry.

"Honey, where's the hot sauce?"
"In the door, right in front of your face."
"No, I already looked there. It's not in here."
(Sound of wife coming to the refrigerator, sighing heavily)
"Here it is." (Handing me the hot sauce 0.13 seconds after arriving at the open refrigerator)

I have been certified completely un-blind by the DMV, so it is obvious to me that she has these things ingeniously hidden

29

somewhere and then pulls a David Copperfield when she steps in front of me to retrieve the obviously hidden item, magically making it seem as if I am a doofus and it was right in front of my nose the whole time. I have no idea why she does that, but she's good at it. She could have her own gig in Vegas.

Anyway, the second lesson we learned this Easter is to count the eggs before you hide them. If we had done that, we would at least have some idea of how many are still missing, because we have no idea where they were all hidden. That brings us to the third lesson we learned: Be careful who you have doing the egg hiding.

My wife and mother-in-law had spent the night before Easter filling the plastic eggs with candy, and as previously stated, neglecting to keep a count. On Easter morning, we all woke up, had breakfast, and headed for church. Not really one for a lot of churchin', my father-in-law volunteered to stay behind and play the part of the Easter Bunny. It had been on-again, off-again rain in the early morning, and it was not clear which direction the weather was headed, so to be safe he opted to hide half of the eggs inside the house, and half of them outside. He did a very thorough job. The only problem was that apparently, as soon as an egg was hidden, its location was immediately erased from his memory.

Well, we got home from church and the kids immediately went at it, gathering as many eggs as they could while running at top speed. It was like watching a polo match without the horses or giant croquet mallets. Little colorful eggs getting kicked everywhere by children too excited to slow down long enough to actually pick them up on the first try.

When we had seemingly run out of places to look, the kids finally slowed down enough that we thought we could get a rough count of the findings.

"How many have we found?"

"I'm not sure. I don't trust the boys' math."

"How many did we make?"

"I don't know. A lot."

"Dad, how many did you hide?"

"All of them."

"No, I mean, how many total? The number."

"I have no idea."

"Do you think we got them all?"

"I have no idea."

"Does this look like how many we made?"

"I can't tell. They're all open now so it looks like twice as many."

After some conferencing by my wife and her mom, and some rough guesses as to how many the kids had found, and some unanswered questions to the hider remaining unanswered, we decided we had probably not found all of them. The kids were already knee-deep in candy, so they didn't really care, and we were getting hungry, so the Easter egg hunt unofficially ended with some debate about whether or not it was really finished.

I am here today to tell you that it was not.

We had rounded up and bagged all of the kids' candy after they had devoured as much as they could get away with, and put it in the pantry for safekeeping and future orderly distribution. Later that day, however, the kids were a little too quiet upstairs and I went to investigate. I found them sitting silently around a pile of plastic egg shells and empty candy wrappers, chocolate smeared on their faces, dazed looks in their eyes, just one or two milligrams of sucrose away from three simultaneous diabetic comas. They had stumbled upon a previously unexplored section of the game room, and came up with two or three eggs each. So much for dinner.

The next morning as I was heading out the door to go to work, I found about six neighborhood kids in my front yard shrubbery. Most of them scattered like roaches when the light comes on, but the few brave souls who didn't make a break for it informed me that a kid on his way to school had noticed a plastic Easter egg under one of our whatchamacallit bushes, and upon further investigation, had apparently hit the mother lode. It wasn't too long before we had nine or ten kids searching our front yard and by all accounts, doing quite well for themselves. My apologies to their teachers that day!

After work that evening, I made a concerted sweep of both the front and back yards and came up with another basket-full of eggs that had gone undiscovered the previous morning. Much to the boy's dismay, those went into the trash under the guise of candy going bad if it stays outside too long, what with all the ants and ticks and fleas and whatnot. Everything except any mini Reese's Peanut Butter Cups, of course. Those don't go bad, and need to go into Daddy's tummy.

Well, I thought that was that. I had surely found them all.

I am here today to tell you that I had not.

The next evening I mowed the grass. The front lawn was uneventful, but the back lawn was downright exciting. In a surprising and painful kind of way.

About midway through the back lawn I ran over what I can only guess were two or three candy-filled plastic Easter eggs that had somehow remained hidden through all the various searches. If you have never hit a plastic Easter egg with a lawn mower blade spinning at 3600 RPM, I can assure you it is eventful.

Any chocolate that was in the eggs was instantly vaporized into a cloud of shiny gold and silver tinfoil dust. The plastic egg shells splintered into roughly 8000 individual shards of pastel-colored shrapnel and assaulted my shins and ankles with a fury that any military superpower would envy. Luckily, this all happened very quickly, so the other projectiles were away from the energy source and heading for their targets before the egg shell shrapnel had dropped me fully to the ground. It was the jelly beans that were the real weapon. Thankfully, I only took a direct hit from one of them, and it was on the side of my shoe where it was only able to cause major damage to one of the bones in my foot. The rest of the jelly beans dispersed from the bottom of the mower at about 400 MPH in all directions. Thankfully, our wooden picnic table took the majority of the beans heading toward the house, saving our sliding glass door from certain death. Many of the others were slowed slightly below lethal velocity by ricocheting off of nearby toys, trees, and bushes, but one or two of them got away clean and had a straight shot at the fence.

There are at least two holes in the fence that I'm pretty sure were not there prior to the jelly bean Claymore mine touching off under my mower. I'm pretty sure at least one of the high-velocity treats hit the neighbor's dog... or one of their kids. I heard a high-pitched yelp, anyway. I would have investigated further, but I was down and crawling for cover.

The moral of the story is simple: If you're going to hide eggs, people, keep an accurate count! And a map! And shin guards.

Besides my injuries, and possible unknown injuries to our neighbor's pet or offspring, I have one more real concern. We know for a fact that there were eighteen hardboiled eggs that the kids colored, and we have only accounted for thirteen of them.

We are just praying they are all outside. We'll find out soon enough.

Mother's Day, Kinda
May 5, 2010

This Mother's Day, I went above and beyond the call of duty and scored the best gift any husband has ever given any wife and mother of three. That's right… Tickets to the Demolition Derby! For me… and my dad… and two of our three boys.

What's that you say? "What kind of Mother's Day gift is *that*?"

Funny… That's exactly what my wife said.

OK, here's what happened. A long time ago, I explained what a demolition derby was to my boys. Because their veins are coursing with my DNA, their eyes lit up at the mere mention of cars crashing into each other. They were almost unrestrained in their enthusiasm as I described how tow-trucks, tractors, and even giant forklifts remove the cars that can't move anymore. And I had to peel them off the ceiling when I hit them with the best part… No mufflers, and sometimes, the cars catch on fire. It was love at first description.

"When can we go, Daddy?"
"We'll go the next time there is a demolition derby anywhere around here," I promised.

So, when I spotted the billboard proclaiming "Demolition Derby – May 9th" at the Dixon May Fair, it was obvious what I needed to do. I rushed home, got on Ticketmaster.com, and procured four tickets. Son Number Three is too young, so it was me and the first two, and my dad, since that happens to be his birthday. What better birthday gift for any American male than an evening watching total automotive chaos?

Beaming with pride at what an outstanding father I was, I triumphantly relayed the news of my ingenious purchase to my wife, to which she responded simply, "That's Mother's Day."

Since I am such a genius, I assumed she was worried about the fact that I was taking my dad, and leaving my mom home alone. So, I replied, "That's OK, my mom won't want to go."

I am an idiot.

After narrowly ducking a flying saucepan, I realized where she was going with that comment. Damn you, mouth! Quit instantly repeating everything the brain comes up with. Give it some time!

Since the tickets were non-refundable, and more importantly, the boys REALLY need to see a demolition derby, I had to think fast. But as it turns out, it's hard to think fast about much else when you're trying to dodge cookware.

After I made my escape to the garage, I applied steady pressure to my head wound, and began to formulate a plan. The tickets were paid for. No going back, there… Only one way to play it… spin it.

When I was relatively certain that my wife was no longer within arm's reach of any pots or pans, I made my move. I kindly explained that if she had given me the chance to finish the story of my incredible purchase, she would have known that the demolition derby was at night.

"You're going to keep the kids up late on a school night?"
"Let's stay focused here, honey."

Since the derby was at night, we would obviously have the entire day to celebrate her Mother's Day any way she wanted. Then, in the late afternoon, I would whisk away two of her three children for the evening, leaving her with only the smallest child of the bunch to tend to. That, in and of itself, is the greatest gift I could give her for her special day, because when you spend all day refereeing three boys, suddenly only having one is tantamount to a vacation. Really, what I had purchased for her was a Mother's Day vacation package.

Hello! Does it get any better than that? You're welcome!

She's still not speaking to me.

I'll bet for a while there, my wife probably thought that giving birth to three boys meant she would only be looking after three boys. No such luck, honey. I am most certainly the fourth boy in the equation. Like the other three, I have wild ideas, and rarely consult the family calendar. But unlike the other three, I have a credit card.

Happy Mother's Day, sweetheart. I love you. Please put down that skillet.

Mother's Day Done Better
May 4, 2011

If you have been following my weekly ramblings for any length of time, you might recall the tale of my impeccable handling of last Mother's Day.

I had skillfully purchased tickets to a demolition derby that happened to be scheduled on the same day that America was holding Mother's Day. The derby promoters refused my requests to move the event up a day, so I was forced to explain to my wife why it would be a good thing for me to take the boys away to a car smashing event on her special day. To add a slight level of difficulty, I had to explain my reasoning while dodging cookware being thrown at my head.

I broke the news of my inadvertent double-booking a week or so before Mother's Day. By "broke the news," I of course mean that she told me what I had done. Then she threw a saucepan at me. Anyway, she was able to calm down in a day or three, and finally saw the error in her initial reaction, or so I thought. She acquiesced and agreed that the gift of relative solitude (I was leaving her with Son Number Three while the other two went to the derby with me) that I had so thoughtfully provided her was indeed a fine Mother's Day gift from a loving husband. A few days later she even helped me figure out what the boys could get her for Mother's Day, since their dad obviously had no clue.

Going so far as to tell me that she had found an "easy and fun" way to have the boys make her gifts, she presented me with the news that I would be going to our local home improvement store on the coming Saturday morning. They were having a kid's craft event for Mother's Day, where the kids could make their mothers a flower pot holder. Better yet, it was free!

My initial reaction was, "Oh, OK, great. That should be fun."

I am a stupid, stupid man. Obviously it was a trap. A trap of retribution.

Off I drove with the boys on Saturday morning, oblivious to my real situation. Fortunately for me, Son Number Three was deemed too young to come to this event as well, so he stayed home with mom. I am convinced that is the only reason why I made it out of there alive. I barely made it through the ordeal with two boys, but adding the third youngest one would have surely been the coup de grace.

It started off innocently enough. We were greeted by teenage store employees who outfitted the boys with kid-size orange store aprons with their names written on the front in black Sharpie marker, which they thought were really cool. Then they handed us our flower pot holder kits, and invited us to pick any open spot at one of the many workbenches set up for the occasion. That's where things began to go south.

My first question caught them off guard. "Where are the kid's workbenches?" I asked.
"Those are the kid's workbenches, sir."
"Why are there hammers on the workbenches?"
"To hammer the nails, sir."
"Nails!?!"
"Yes, sir. They're included in your kit. You're supposed to glue the joints and then nail them together."
"Glue!?!"
"Yes, sir. Is there a problem?"
"Is it real glue and real nails?"
"Of course, sir."
"Then, yes. We have a problem. You mean to tell me that these things don't just snap together like Legos? You want my four-year-old to be swinging a hammer?"
"Well, we don't think they should swing them, so much as just tap the nails into place."
"Have you ever met a four-year-old boy?"

Oh, well. There was no going home empty handed, so to the workbench we went.

Two minutes later, as I had predicted, I was refereeing a tug-of-war over an erupting bottle of Elmer's wood glue and desperately dodging the claw ends of two fast moving hammers.

I found myself holding miniature nails upright between my thumb and index finger, praying the first blow would be to the head of the nail, and not to the head of the dad, or to the fingers, hand, arm, or face of the dad.

I spent a considerable amount of time fighting back the onslaught of excess glue with almost an entire roll of paper towels, all the while trying to decipher the steadily more glue-ridden assembly instructions before my boys had nailed or glued something to the wrong spot.

It was a lot like trying to do a crossword puzzle while trapped inside a spinning dryer full of open glue bottles and claw hammers. And nails.

After we had somehow managed to complete two fairly intact and somewhat recognizable flower pot stands, and the employees had found me some extra-large gauze pads and an ice pack, we made our way to the garden section to find some nice Mother's Day flowers to adorn our new creations.

I foolishly thought that this would be the easy part. How hard could it be to find a couple of small flowers in pots? Ha! You have obviously never shopped for flowers with my boys! Neither had I.

Apparently my children are not very impressed with ordinary, everyday, run-of-the-mill flowers. They seem to only be attracted to the high-dollar exotic breed flowers. No azaleas or daisies for their mommy! No, they just had to buy mom the Madagascar crouching tiger orchid and the greenhouse-raised

Turkish gold river lilac, each costing about the same amount as an entire pallet of rose bushes, and both guaranteed to last about 1.7 hours under our family's expert horticultural care.

Again, I couldn't go home with two boys telling their already emotionally iffy mother that Daddy wouldn't let them buy the pretty flowers for her, so out came the credit card. Ka-ching.

The whole experience hurt. Physically, financially, emotionally, you name it, it hurt. All things considered, I think I would have rather gone to the mall, and you know how I feel about the mall.

When we got home, my wife gave me a sly smile and said, "How did the project go, sweetie?"

I knew right then and there that this had been payback for my demolition derby scheduling blunder and lack of believable spin on the reason why. As I went to get a fresh ice pack, I vowed not to make that same mistake again. She is way too smart for me.

True to my vow, this year I learned from last year's mistakes. This year I won't fall into any of those traps. This year there is absolutely no way for me to get into any trouble!

This year, I have planned absolutely nothing for Mother's Day.

Smooth sailing ahead!

Right?

Resolutions
January 5, 2011

My wife had been after me all week to tell her what my New Year's resolutions were, and apparently, "I don't have any," was not an acceptable answer, so I was forced to find some. I did some quick internet research and came up with a list of the most popular resolutions in America. Not wanting to appear like I was slacking off, I have adopted all of them. Bring it on, 2011!

Spend more time with family and friends
Since the only two things I do are work and hang out with my family and friends, the only way to accomplish this resolution was to quit my job. Done.

Go to the gym more
OK, let's not start talking crazy. I modified this one slightly to fit my lifestyle. I resolved to drive past the gym at least twice a week. If I go the long way to 7-Eleven, I can go by the gym on my way to get my 94-oz soda. Baby steps, people!

Lose weight
I am all about this resolution. I have been keeping my eye on the new MacBook Air, and I think it's time to pull the trigger on that bad boy. That should get rid of about five pounds compared to my old Dell.

Quit smoking
I don't know if I'm going to be able to do this one, and frankly, I really don't understand why I need to. I mean, what's better than ribs? Answer… nothing. Still, I guess I could rotisserie more chickens or something like that. I'll have to think about this one some more.

Enjoy life more

Uh… hello? Didn't they pay attention to the first one? I just quit my job. This one is kind of redundant, don't you think?

Quit drinking

No problem there. This one requires no action on my part. I only drink beer, and everyone knows, beer doesn't count. It's more of a food group than a beverage, really. They can't possibly mean beer, can they? I mean, what would I drink while I was smoking? Or rotisserie-ing?

Get out of debt

This one may be a little tricky, since I just quit my job, but I have at least resolved to stop taking payday loans to cover my gambling losses. That should help. I will, instead, borrow money from friends and relatives. That should cut down on my principal and interest payments significantly.

Learn a new language

I have actually been meaning to do this for quite a while, so this resolution thing should really be the boost I need. I am going to learn to speak Number Three. I am constantly having to ask Son Number One and Son Number Two what the heck Number Three just said. Everyone in our house can understand our youngest son, except me. My wife will really appreciate it when I finally crack the code! It should also really help him when he's trying to tell me stuff like, "My head is stuck," or "You're sitting on me."

Help others

This one sounded like a lot of work, and appears to involve talking to other people, so I decided to modify it slightly. I have resolved to give my sons 30% fewer smart-ass answers to their questions. That should help them learn more actual facts, and should satisfy this category.

Stick to a budget

Budgets have never really worked out for me, and since I am unemployed now, the idea just seems silly. I mean, how can I have a budget when I don't have a paycheck? Hello! So, I have modified this one to be "Stick to a system." Namely, my horse picking system at the track. I figure without any future paychecks, I will need to really buckle down and get serious at the track if I'm going to feed the family.

Find my soul mate
This one required some modification. For starters, since I already have a wife, finding my soul mate might involve a messy divorce. Plus, one of the main reasons I got married in the first place was so that I could stop dating. In light of these considerations, I have decided instead to find my soul mate of beer. My beer mate, if you will. Yes, that one perfect beer that compliments everything in my new and improved life. I don't expect the search to be easy. On the contrary, I think this quest may take a lifetime, but I'm willing to put that kind of time in for such an important resolution.

Find a better job
Again... hello? I just quit my last job. Don't they even pay attention to their own lists? I have found a better job; namely, no job. Duh!

Be less stressed
Let's see, here... I'm an unemployed guy on a quest to find his beer mate. This one should not be a problem.

On second thought, when I presented this list to my wife, she looked a little stressed. That sometimes has a way of coming around to bite me, so the "Be less stressed" one might be a little more difficult than I thought.

She keeps muttering something that sounds like, "You quit your what?" and her face seems a little redder than normal. Maybe she should think about quitting her job and going on a quest to find her wine mate. I'll suggest that to her. That might get me some extra points in the "Help others" category, too.

I can't figure out why she seems so upset. After all, this was her idea.

3

Men vs. Women

People who like to spout about the "equality of the sexes" are wildly misguided. The sexes are not by any stretch of the imagination equal. They are, at best, complimentary. For instance, men exist to help light things on fire, and women exist to help bandage men's burn wounds.

Hot Chicks and Cool Dudes
July 7, 2008

One of the main differences between men and women can be seen in the simple truth about ambient temperature. Men are comfortable in a thirty-degree temperature range, and the range is the same for all men. From 56 degrees Fahrenheit to 86, men will do just fine. Some may be a little sweatier or chillier than others, but no one is complaining. This range is hardwired in the male DNA and stays the same from birth until death.

Women, on the other hand, are comfortable in only a three-degree range, and not only does that range vary widely from woman to woman, but throughout the course of an individual woman's day, week, month, year, and lifespan, it will jump all over the board.

These are indisputable facts. You just can't argue with science. This disparity in the comfort zones of the sexes invariably leads to problems when men and women attempt to share an office, car, home, bed, table at a restaurant, tent, etc. The issue is most often solved by adjusting the temperature to fit the female's needs. As long as the three-degree range is still falling in the male comfort zone, everyone gets along. If there are two or more women sharing the same space, the inevitable problem is usually solved with layers. It is not uncommon to visit an office where the secretary in the blouse with the personal electric desk fan is working right alongside the HR manager in the parka with the personal electric space heater.

Financial issues can arise from this problem when men and women get married and buy a house that contains a thermostat. Men will do some rudimentary math, and pick one temperature to keep the house livable, foolishly assuming that this temperature will be acceptable for the entire season. Little do they know that the temperature they picked will not even be acceptable for an entire seven minutes. Women who normally complain that the clock radio is too complicated can decipher a thirty-eight-button, eleven-switch thermostat in a matter of minutes and operate any home's A/C system like they were seated at a NASA control center. In many cases the temperature swings during the day are so violent that a man can actually see the money being sucked out of the double-pane windows.

I think the temperature issue is a physical manifestation of a psychological difference in the sexes. Women are genetically programmed to worry about more things than men are. I have no idea why, but again, you can't argue with science. When women have no life-threatening situations to deal with, they will inevitably begin to search out things to be concerned about, often making things up to fret over. Hair, weight, money, age, wrinkles, relationships with friends, relationships with co-workers, me-time, us-time, down time, play dates, date night, pre-partum, partum, post-partum, carpet, color palates, window treatments, balanced diets, safety recalls, consumer reports, outdoor tableware, biological clocks, school districts, undercooked poultry, guest lists, footwear, closet organization, furniture, pediatricians, and the list goes on and on. And on.

With men, pretty much twenty-nine days out of the month if the cars are running OK and the house isn't on fire, it's all good.

So I hypothesize that women, being less comfortable inside about all the little things in life, try to micro-manage the external temperature settings to feel more comfortable outside. A way to gain some measure of control over their surroundings when life seems otherwise wildly out of control. Either that, or it's a hormone thing and they actually are less comfortable. What do I know?

Boys vs. Girls
November 16, 2011

The other day we had some friends and their kids over for one last backyard barbeque hurrah before old man winter puts the kibosh on that sort of thing. As will happen in the classic American barbeque scenario, the men ended up out on the back patio standing around the grill holding beers and watching the kids play, and the women ended up in the kitchen and living room drinking wine and complaining that the men were not watching the kids properly. At least that's what we assumed they were talking about, since no man in the history of the classic American barbeque scenario has ever been foolish enough to go inside and inquire.

So, as the men huddled around the grill, and the women did whatever the women do inside the house, the boys were having a great time on our play structure, playing some sort of fort/swing/cricket/dodgeball/jai-alai hybrid game that continually evolved with rotating team members and flexible rules, as kid's games often do. It was hard to follow, but the kids seemed to always know what was going on. As near as the dads could figure, if you got hit with the batted Wiffle ball while in motion on one of the swings, you had to jump off the swing, climb up onto the play structure platform, and throw soccer balls at the guys with the bats. If you got hit with a soccer ball, you had to drop your bat and quickly get up to the platform and go down the slide before you were hit with one of your own Wiffle balls. If you caught the Wiffle ball, you had unlimited bomb powers… Like I said, it was hard to follow, but it was mighty entertaining.

A few times during the action one or two of the moms stuck their head out the sliding glass door to inquire about the safety of the game, but we assured them that Wiffle balls are mostly harmless, and the kids were just having fun, so everything was OK. They seemed unconvinced, but didn't push the issue.

The game ran its natural course, lasting the standard ten to fifteen minutes of semi-coherent action, then devolving into small roving bands of children sort of still playing that game, but kinda playing something else. It eventually morphed into one small soccer game and a separate swinging height contest, both of which were far less entertaining for the adults. Just when we thought all the good action was over, a bright spot could be seen shining through the haze. One of the seven-year-olds seemed to have a quest. He had found our "Big Wheel" tricycle. If you're my age, I'm sure you rode one as a kid. The multi-colored all-plastic design, with the low-slung seat set back between the small-diameter wide rear wheels and the handlebars high above the large-diameter skinny front wheel with the direct-coupled foot pedals. An American classic. The Radio Flyer of the '70s kids.

Our young beacon of hope had found the Big Wheel and was in the process of holding it by one of the handlebars while walking up the play structure's slide, dragging the Big Wheel behind him. We dads thought that was fairly impressive, since Big Wheels, despite being made of plastic, are pretty heavy for a seven-year-old. He made it all the way to the top of the slide and onto the platform with his load, and then began getting into position.

The slide is plastic with wooden side rails, and only about twenty inches wide. He put the large front wheel in the middle of the slide heading downhill, but since the Big Wheel's rear axle was too wide for both back wheels to fit on the slide, he had to cockeye the back end and put only one back wheel on the slide, with the plastic undercarriage near the other wheel resting up on the wooden side rail.

Quickly assessing the situation, using the innate risk versus reward software that men hone and refine in our brains over our lifetimes, we dads concluded that the drag from the plastic undercarriage on the wooden rail would offset the low-friction rolling wheels, keeping the rider at a relatively safe and manageable speed. He would need to pull up hard on the handlebars for the launch off the end of the slide onto the lawn, and then cut it hard to the right to avoid a head-on with the fence, but he could definitely pull it off. His worst-case scenario was a few scrapes and splinters. Assessment: Totally worth it.

Approving of the venture, and eagerly anticipating the first test run, we watched as he worked out how to get onto the Big Wheel without having it start down without him. He was just making his way into the seat when a whole gaggle of moms came bursting from the living room and kitchen onto the patio, shouting, "No!!!"

We turned around in surprise to face the horde of naysaying mothers, shocked to see them glaring at us with icy, dagger-throwing eyes.

"It's alright," I said, trying to calm the group down. "That plastic frame isn't going to hurt the wood."

As it turns out, that wasn't what they were concerned about at all.

As we listened intently to the ladies' concerns, and I watched the young boy's mom dismantling what would have been a perfectly mostly safe and totally awesome test run, a thought occurred to me. This is why there aren't too many female test pilots.

When a girl looks at a steep hill, she thinks to herself... I honestly have no idea what she thinks to herself.

When a boy looks at a steep hill, he thinks to himself, "You know, if I was on something that had wheels, I could go really fast down this sucker!"

50

When a girl looks at a bike, or a skateboard, or a scooter, she probably thinks to herself, "That looks like a fun and effective mode of transportation," or something like that.

When a boy looks at anything with wheels on it, he thinks to himself, "You know, I bet that thing would go faster if the back end of it was on fire."

Boys are doing math at a young age, constantly putting two and two together. Play structure plus Big Wheel equals fun. Pool plus roof of house equals bigger splash. Firecracker plus anything else equals awesome.

I have tried, but it seems to be a very hard concept to explain to my wife. I just don't think women really get it.

He totally would have made it!

4

Our World Today

My parents had it easy. They didn't have to deal with cell phones, computer hackers, or microscopic watch batteries. Of course, they did have to deal with me.

Batteries Are Draining Me
December 5, 2008

If you have kids in the house, then somewhere in that house you no doubt run a small side business warehousing batteries. Depending on how many kids and toys you have, you may actually own more batteries than some third-world countries. I know for a fact that I own more AAs than Bangladesh.

In the good old days of my youth, my toys took only one size battery. The 9-volt. It had opposite terminals on top and you had to plug it into the vinyl-coated contacts at the end of two thin red and white wires stuffed into the battery compartment of your walkie-talkie or radio-controlled race car. When you took the old battery out it was always a gamble on whether you would rip those wires right out of the toy, because the used 9-volt always managed to weld itself to the contacts. You could check to make sure the old battery was really dead by putting the contacts on your tongue. Everyone who has ever done it remembers vividly the first time they put a brand new 9-volt on their tongue. The cattle prod-like shock across your taste buds and the lingering metallic flavor is unforgettable. Good times!

There were only two other sizes of battery besides the 9-volt in my youth. The D-cell, which went in standard flashlights, and the gigantic, slightly smaller than a brick, "lantern battery" with the two cone-shaped spiral spring contacts on top. They went in the molded plastic flashlight with the seven-inch-diameter lens and integral suitcase handle that every family had for camping or emergencies. It was six volts instead of nine, but no one ever thought about putting that one on their tongue! They always seemed to last for a sum total of eight and a half minutes in the three hundred-pound flashlight before it would begin to get dimmer and dimmer. At that point your parents or grandparents would let you turn it on and keep it on so you could stare at the faint glow from the bulb as long as you could to try to pinpoint the exact second that the battery went completely dead. Who needs a PlayStation?

I rarely see the 9-volt or the eighteen-pound brick nowadays. They have been replaced by approximately eighty-seven other models, shapes and voltages. The clear winner is the AA, which seems to have held the top spot for a long time now. I remember as a bachelor being indignant when I got my fist TV remote that took AAAs. "Why do I need these? The AAs works just fine! Now I have to stock two kinds of small batteries." Little did I know, that was only the beginning. I got married, had kids, and somewhere along the line, someone brought thirteen tons of toys into my home. With the exception of one old-timer wooden train, each and every toy requires batteries. Our portable plastic baby fence takes batteries. We have a wooden puzzle that takes batteries. We have stuffed animals, cribs, and bikes that take batteries. And we have books that take batteries. Now come on! The last thing in the world that is supposed to require batteries is a book.

The manufacturers of the battery-operated books and some of the other toys have taken things one step further. In a creepy effort to make their products popular, or at least seem popular, the toys will actually try to get the kid's attention back if they stop playing with them. When you put them down or stop turning pages for a minute, they call out to the child, "Turn the page to hear more," or, "Elmo's lonely, play with me." Why don't they just be honest and have the toy say, "Excuse me son, sales are down in North America. We would like this product to hold your interest for another three-tenths of a second so your mommy will distinguish it as being special and purchase one for your cousin."

Until recently, my wife and I had a nice run where we were only stocking AAs, AAAs, C-cells, D-cells, and the occasional 9-volt. Granted, we have to buy AAs and C's by the pallet, pretty much weekly, but at least we only had to inventory five different kinds. That has all changed now. My sons just got their first set of walkie-talkies. Did their super-cool new Transformers Walkie-Talkie set come with 9-volts like mine did when I was their age? No. They came with calculator batteries. You know the kind. They go in your car's keychain remote. They look like a dime or a nickel. And they are from Hell.

When you go to the regular battery section at the store it is a straightforward affair. Need AAs, there they are. When you go to the calculator battery section of the store you had better bring some water and a snack, because you're going to be there for a while. For reasons known only to the battery company engineers, they felt the need to designate them with a letter and a number. C124 or A534. Probably because there are only twenty-six letters in the alphabet, and they anticipated a need for at least three thousand unique sizes. Besides having an almost infinite amount of diameter and thickness combinations, they have cross-references between the model numbers printed in microscopic writing on the packages. It's like a fun little treasure hunt where you have to find one dime in a pile of two hundred dimes. The D435 is compatible with the A534, the F129, as well as the H245, but not the D534 or the F534.

Just in case it was too simple, the battery companies' marketing teams went ahead and designated some of them as "medical"

54

and put the universal Red Cross symbol on the package. If I need an H432 for my kid's toy, and it comes in "medical" and plain, which should I choose? Will the "medical" one last longer, or will it immediately recognize that it is not powering a Life Alert necklace, and fail to work at all?

The good news is that the calculator batteries come in packs of one, and they cost $9.78 each on average. Our new walkie-talkie set takes four per unit, so if my math is correct, when the batteries run out in both units it should only cost me $3240.87 and six hours of my time cross-referencing in the battery aisle. That is sooooo much better than the forty cents and two minutes it would have taken me if they were AAs.

If you'll excuse me, I have to go take the folks from Energizer and Duracell off my Christmas card list.

Assembly Required
December 1, 2010

My oldest son, Number One, recently celebrated his sixth birthday, and received a transforming robot "kit" from his grandparents. On the outside of the exciting multi-colored box it showed the robot, standing proud and looking for adventure, and it displayed the two other "modes" that he could turn into, namely an airplane and a scorpion. It was solar powered and motorized to move on its own. The outside of the box looked like any six-year-old's dream. The inside of the box was another matter entirely.

We knew there was "assembly required," because one of the fun features of the toy was that you got to "build it yourself." I was excited about having a father-son activity where he could gain experience building something mechanical. He tore open the box and spread the contents out and on the table. I took one look at the inventory, and in as calm a voice as I could muster, asked him to put his hands on his head and slowly back away from the toy. The plan had changed. The largest thing in the box, by a wide margin, was the instruction manual. That's never a good sign.

There were three plastic bags containing screws so small, you could lose them all at once with a good sneeze. There were tiny plastic gears, a half-inch in diameter, with little drive shafts, no thicker than a paper clip. There was a one-inch-square solar panel connected to the smallest motor I have ever seen. The motor was no more than 3/8 of an inch long and less than 1/4 inch round. It was tethered to the solar panel with two four-inch-long wires roughly the thickness of human hairs.

There were two rafts of plastic parts, containing roughly eighty parts each, all still attached to their spider web of molded plastic anchor points. Some of the parts were so small I was really not

56

sure where I needed to cut to get them free. "Is that a part that I need, or is that the piece I'm supposed to cut off? I can't tell!"

I was flabbergasted by how complicated and technical this child's toy was, so I took another look at the box. It advertised that the toy was for ages ten to adult, with the added caveat that no child under four was to get within a fifty-foot radius of any of the small parts. I agreed wholeheartedly with the lower age limit, but not because I was worried about a choking incident. There was no part of the entire assembly large enough to choke a child. An infant could have swallowed the motor whole, no problem. I figured the warning was simply to give you a fighting chance of ending up with all the pieces you needed to make it work. To that end, it should really have read, "no child under eighteen."

I took serious issue with the ten and up rating, however. I am thirty-eight years old, I have an engineering degree, and I have been designing and assembling mechanical apparatuses professionally for over twenty years, and I had grave reservations about my ability to complete the task. I contend that there is no ten-year-old on this planet with the patience, forethought, dexterity, motor skills, mechanical knowledge, or even the proper tools to assemble one of these things.

There would be no father-son activity today. Involving a six-year-old in this project would have been like asking Mike Tyson to tune your Stradivarius violin. Wrong guy for the job. I locked the door to the room and went to work.

Step 1 had me pressing the pinion gear onto the motor shaft. The gear was half the size of a pencil eraser, and the motor's shaft was the diameter of a gnat's eyelash. It was a "press fit" so the gear wouldn't slip on the shaft, and I had to push it down as hard as my fingers could press to get it on, without accidentally bending the miniscule shaft. Ten-year-olds were disqualified on the first step.

In steps 12 through 18, I threaded two of the tiniest wires I have ever seen through an obstacle course of plastic needle-holes, snapping the assembly together as I went, making sure not to sever either of the wires by accidentally pinching them or looking at them the wrong way.

In step 35 I assembled a quadruple-reduction, eight-gear transmission inside a shrouded plastic housing. It was the plastic robot equivalent of the ship in a bottle, only the ship was the size of your fingernail, and the bottle wasn't see-through.

In step 114 I had to go to the garage and find my straight-shaft #0 Phillips head screwdriver in my specialty tool kit. Do you have a straight-shaft #0 Phillips head screwdriver? No? Well, you would have been dead in the water at step 114.

In step 254 I assembled a double offset cam and linkage system that would have made Leonardo da Vinci weep with joy.

In step 316 I wept. Not with joy.

In step 496 I split an atom.

In step 513 I snapped together the last piece, and marveled at how small it was.

The entire robot, tip to toe, was only three and a half inches tall. It took me an hour and a half to assemble it. That's almost a half-hour per inch.

I unlocked the door and went out to display my accomplishment with pride.

"What took you so long?" was the only response from my wife.

I went back in and re-locked the door until I calmed down.

When I had regained my composure, I came back out and handed Number One his new toy. He and his middle brother, Number Two, went outside to set it in the sun, and cheered as they watched it walk down the sidewalk. Then they brought it inside and tore one of its legs off while calmly discussing who should be allowed to play with it next. It lasted seven and a half minutes.

Maybe we don't need that leg for airplane mode...

This was quite a "toy." I was just barely old enough to assemble it, and my boys were at least a decade too young to play with it. I think the box should really read, "Must be a forty-five-year-old aerospace engineer to assemble, and must be at least thirty-five to operate."

I'll give it one thing, though. At least it didn't require any batteries.

Losing Our Remote Control
August 17, 2011

Our whole world changed this morning. Our oldest son learned how to use the remote control. Now, granted, he is only a few months away from being seven years old, so before you accuse him of being of below-average intelligence, allow me to explain. He already knew how to use the remote control, in the sense that he could turn the TV on and change the channel. We actually taught him that at an early age out of a desire to sleep in. Our boys naturally get up much earlier than my wife and I really want to, so it was either teach him how to turn on the Disney channel in the morning by himself, or we would need to go to bed earlier. We chose the TV option.

I know some of you out there are now thinking, "How much TV do these people let their kids watch?" I can assure you it is way less than nine hours per day. We actually tried other forms of pre-parental-consciousness morning activities, such as Legos, sword fighting, and wrestling, but watching TV was the only thing that didn't consistently end in a loud argument or an even louder head injury.

Up until this morning, Son Number One was able to turn on the TV in our upstairs game room and change the channel to 303 for Disney. At 6:00 in the morning, the Disney channel is a safe bet to be appropriate for all age groups. Up until this morning, this was a satisfactory morning activity for Sons One, Two and Three. Up until this morning, I didn't have to worry about what they might see on the TV screen.

That has all changed now.

We have a whole host of children's shows that we record on the DVR (that stands for Digital Video Recorder, for those of you over 50 years old) for the kids to choose from when we parents

60

are awake and able to operate the menu to get them going. Apparently, Son Number One has been paying close attention to us when we navigate the recorded shows menu, because that's exactly what he did this morning.

Our soon-to-be-seven-year-old powered on the big downstairs TV that has its own remote, changed the TV's input to the DVR, switched remotes, navigated his way through the main menu to the recorded shows menu, scrolled through the list until he found Tarzan, selected it, scrolled through the list of eight Tarzan episodes that were recorded, found the sequel to the episode they had watched the night before, selected it, found "play" among the list of options, and fast-forwarded through the commercials to the beginning of the show.

My wife silently witnessed the entire event from the kitchen, and after she picked her jaw up off the counter and regained some amount of composure, she came to find me upstairs to tell me that we had a big problem. "Number One can work the TV."

"I know."

"No, you don't understand. He just played Tarzan from the DVR."

"He did what?!?"

Now, our shock and apprehension about this new skill our son has developed has nothing to do with Tarzan, or any other show we recorded for the boys. Those are fine. Even the commercials on the Disney channel are pretty harmless, although, my boys really want me to buy an ultrasonic noise maker that is supposed to keep pests like deer and raccoons out of our garden. I'm having trouble getting them to come to grips with the fact that we don't really need that in our suburban backyard. They're pretty insistent though. I think it's because on the commercial it shows the imaginary semi-circles of sound emanating from the cheesy-looking green plastic device. I have tried to explain that they will not be able to see - or even hear - the sound in real life, but they're not convinced that I know what I'm talking about.

Anyway, our apprehension about Son Number One's remote control skills has nothing to do with his shows. It has everything to do with our shows. We record a lot of police and detective dramas, and I don't have to tell you that today's shows are over the top. If our kids get curious one morning and end up witnessing an *NCIS* autopsy scene, or catch some of the dialogue from *Law and Order: SVU*, I'm not sure even a team of professional child psychologists could reverse that damage.

Now, AT&T U-Verse has already envisioned this problem, and they were kind enough to include parental controls software with the DVR. Apparently, we could simply set up a password, and block access to any of the shows we choose, thereby protecting young impressionable minds from adult language, descriptions of violent crimes, and the dissected spleens of unfortunate sailors. Sounds great in theory, but there are a few problems here in reality.

I'm not sure there's a really delicate way to put this, so I'll just come out and say it. We're afraid if we add any more steps, we won't be able to operate the TV ourselves. We already have three remotes, and at the very least, a nine-step process to actually watch a show. One more level of difficulty might very well put us over the top. And don't even get me started on the grandparents! It's like teaching Chinese algebra to a goldfish every time they come over to babysit and need to operate the TV. One more step in that process will not be good.

I guess we could teach Son Number One to help them with the operation of the parental controls, but that seems like a flawed system, somehow...

Maybe we should look at this new development not as a challenge, but as an opportunity to change what we watch and record, moving toward a more wholesome Discovery Channel and History Channel-only type environment. Or maybe abandon the idiot box altogether and move to a books-only lifestyle.

Nah… I think I'll just start hiding the remotes. I'll put them with his shoes. He can never find those.

Hacker Grammar Bad
August 24, 2011

When my sisters and I were growing up, my mom constantly hammered home good grammar and spelling. If we said, "Me and my friends went to the park," we were immediately corrected with, "My friends and I..."

"Ain't" was forbidden to be uttered within a six-block radius of her home, and any misspelled words were underlined for correction before homework was allowed to be returned.

This continued through our high school years, and beyond, into college, and even continues today if I have a rare grammatical slip-up while talking with my mother on the phone. Anyway... When I was sent off into the world with my impeccable grammar and spelling, it started to become clear to me right away why my mother was so insistent on using English correctly. Good grammar is one of the trademarks of polite, civilized, educated society. There is no quicker way to be dismissed in business, or to be discounted as a miscreant, than to not know how you should talk good.

Yet, as with so many annoying things your parents did to you, only after you become a parent yourself do you truly understand the value, and truly appreciate their efforts. Poor grammar offends my very senses, and misspellings jump off the page at me as if they were highlighted. Today, I am riding grammatical herd on my boys, just like my mom did with us. "You didn't throwed the ball, son, you threw it."

And as with all labors of love, many of the fruits of said labors aren't realized until much, much later. My mom could never have known it at the time, but she was helping the next generation fight off computer hackers. Way to go, Mom!

Hackers, as a rule, have atrocious grammar. I'm not sure if this is because they are all phishing from North Korea, China, and Nigeria, and just don't have the lingo down pat, or if they are simply American-born-and-raised ne'er-do-wells, or both. I guess it really doesn't matter, as long as they keep tipping their hand with missing verbs. Here's an example of something I received the other day:

An e-mail from an address that was vaguely official, but not quite, like "manager@creditaccount.com," with a subject line reading, "Your Credit Card Overdue." (Good start, guys!)

Dear Customer,
Your Credit Card is one week overdue.
Below your Card information
Customer 7990682142
Number XXXXX
Card Limit XXXXX
Pay Date 29 Jun 2011
The details are attached to this e-mail.
Please read the financial statement properly.
If you pay debt within 2 days, there will be no extra-charges.
In 2 days $25 late fee and a finance charge will be imposed on your account.
Please do not reply to this email, its automatic mail notification.
Thank you.

The attachment was a zip file titled "account_information.zip," that surely contained a password stealing program or a virus of some flavor.

Now, come on, fellas! How stupid do you think I am? I mean, how hard would it be to find someone who can actually speak and read English to proofread your idiotic fake account alert?

The ridiculousness of it amazes me, but at the same time, it is totally understandable. If they had more smarts, they wouldn't be criminals in the first place. Like the dynamic duo a few years ago that tried to rip an ATM out of the ground with their pickup truck. They attached a chain from their rear bumper to the ATM, and then hit the gas. The ATM stayed put and their bumper ended up on the ground. They had long since sped away from the scene of the almost-crime when the police arrived. The cops simply ran the license plate, found still attached to the bumper that was still attached to the ATM, and drove to their house to pick them up.

For a minute or two, you shake your head and wonder to yourself, "Why didn't they at least retrieve the plate, let alone the bumper and the chain?" But then, the more you think about what they tried to do, and how they tried to do it, you say to yourself, "Of course they left it behind."

The same thing is true, I guess, of communist North Korean hackers. If they had enough smarts to figure out how to do it right, they'd probably already be South Koreans. And if the American computer virtuoso-gone-hacker had an ounce of common sense, he would be writing programs for Microsoft instead of writing worms for the Russian mob.

I have to give the Nigerians a little credit, though. I have been getting scam e-mails from them for over ten years now, and at least they embraced their limitations early on.

"Look, guys, we can't pretend we're from their bank. They'll never buy it. We can't spell, and between all thirty-seven of us in this room, we can't put together one decent sentence. Let's just pretend we're the son of a deposed king from right here in Nigeria. That way the grammar will be excusable. Hold my machete, Motumbo, I'm gonna start typing."

As more and more of our everyday personal financial transactions are handled online, there is a cosmic leveling of the playing field when it comes to something as old-fashioned and fundamental as good grammar and spelling. The bad grammar of the hacker world is really quite handy. If the e-mails in your

66

inbox were customers at a 7-Eleven, the bad grammar is the ski mask. See it, and you know something bad is about to go down.

Now, if you will excuse me, I need to call my mom and thank her. Its cause a her learnin' me right them hackers ain't gonna git me!

5

<u>Parenting</u>

Raising children is the most rewarding experience a couple can have. There is a good reason for that. If there was something even slightly more rewarding, no one would ever bother with the hassle of having kids.

<u>I Have a Dream – A Father's Version</u>
July 8, 2008

Let us not wallow in the valley of despair, I say to you today, my friends. And so even though we face the difficulties of today and tomorrow, I still have a dream. It is a dream deeply rooted in the American dream. It is a Father's Dream.

I have a dream that one day I will be able to sleep in. That one day I will not be woken by the sound of a wooden kitchen spoon banging on my door at 5:30 A.M.

I have a dream that I will one day be able to wear a shirt for more than ten minutes without getting baby spit-up on it.

I have a dream that one day I will not have to watch four effeminate Australians dance poorly and sing about fruit salad and a big red car. That one day I can stop having to sing along with those four effeminate Australians.

I have a dream that my three little boys will one day be able to play with someone else's children without someone going to time out or the emergency room.

I have a dream that my children will someday get up in the middle of the night, go pee, and go right back to bed without waking me up to tell me about it.

I have a dream that someday soon I will be able to walk through my own house barefoot in the dark without fear of plastic dinosaur puncture wounds.

I have a dream that I will no longer have to count to three. That someday I will only need to get to two.

I have a dream that someday I will get into the car and stop finding two-week-old fruit snacks in the leather seats. That I will quit having to vacuum pulverized goldfish crackers out of the floor mats.

I have a dream that one day I will remove my last car seat, never having to contort myself to install it in another car again.

I have a dream that one day my children will travel with only one suitcase each, and they will carry that suitcase themselves. That one day they will not require thirty-two tons of accessories per child.

I have a dream that someday soon I will be able to stand at my toilet and pee without having a little boy come up behind me and try to stick his head between my legs because he thinks it's funny.

I have a dream that one day I will be able to open my own cupboards freely, without first having to Houdini a child-proof plastic locking device. That one day we may be able to have breakables below the five foot line.

I have a dream that someday soon I will be able to set my drink down on the coffee table without a care in the world. That someone somewhere would produce a reliable stain repellant for carpet.

I have a dream that one day I will no longer have to play the "Identify the Foul Smell and its Source" game. That one day, I will no longer stockpile poop-filled diapers in my laundry room until the "odor reducing" container is full enough to go to the trash.

I have a dream that the day will come when I will no longer find any long-forgotten sippy cups of curdled milk underneath my couch.

I have a dream that I will once again be able to eat my whole meal at a restaurant without once uttering the words "inside voice," or, "Please don't stab your brother with your fork."

I have a dream that someday what is on my plate will cease to be much more desirable than what is on his plate. That his green things will stop being "yucky" while mine are "yummy."

I have a dream that one Saturday morning in the future my boys will be able to run into my room and jump on me in bed without one of them kicking me in the goodies.

And when this happens, I will sing:

Free at last! Free at last!
Thank God Almighty, we are free at last!

Because our boys will be growing up and done with all those annoying childhood problems. Teenagers are easier, right?

My Mind is in the Toilet
September 20, 2008

Now that I am a dad, I spend a lot of time thinking about toilets. They seem to have become a central theme in my life. I have a four-year-old and a two-and-a-half-year-old in potty training and that inevitably leads to a lot of concern over commodes.

All activities away from the home now have a toilet element in the planning that sometimes eclipses all other decision making.

- We need to try and go potty before we leave.
- Was it successful?
- Yes. OK we're good for a while.
- No? OK, when was the last time we went potty?
- Will that affect our route to the mall?
- We'd better try again at the mall before we do anything else.
- Where are the toilets in the mall and how will that affect where I park?
- What did we come to the mall for? Was it toilets? I forget.

On road trips I used to stop only when I needed gas and I would choose a gas station based on the price of unleaded. Now I stop at regularly scheduled potty intervals and I choose gas stations on a wide variety of criteria, all having to do with the toilet.

- Does this place have a potty?
- If so, is it in a safe, well lit location?
- If so, does the exterior suggest that the interior will be clean?
- If so, based on past restroom/gas station chain experience, is this place likely to have a diaper changing station (for the six-month-old)?
- If so, does this place also sell gas?

- If so, great! What's that? The gas is sixty-seven dollars per gallon more than the dimly-lit, dirty-looking place across the street? Oh, well!

Once I have picked a bathroom successfully, and we're going in, I now find myself paying much more attention to the lower half of the room. This is due to the proximity of my boys to the floor and their propensity for picking anything up. I'm like a Secret Service agent clearing a hotel's back corridor just seconds ahead of POTUS.

"Yes, I'm in and we have one unsavory character at urinal three, but otherwise clear of civilians, over."

"Wait, we've got something on the floor. Hang on."

"No, it's OK, it's just an empty McDonald's bag."

"We're clear people, let's bring 'em in."

And what is the story with public parks that don't have toilets? The people that build parks know that children will come there, right? They put in nineteen acres of Kentucky bluegrass and keep it mowed and trimmed neater than the fairways at Augusta, but they can't afford to maintain one hole in the ground? What am I paying taxes for? I'm not even asking for toilet paper! I'll bring my own. I always have wipes. Just provide a hole and a seat. This is an especially troubling phenomenon in the newer subdivisions without any mature trees. You never really know how you're going to react in a crisis situation until you have a kid dancing around at your heels saying, "Daddy, Daddy I really need to poop," and you scan the area to discover you are standing on what looks like the surface of the moon. "Hold it" is not a fool-proof option for a three-year-old when you're fifteen minutes from home. Sometimes, you just have to hold your kid over a trash can.

And speaking of wipes, how did we ever live our pre-parental lives without them? I can't even remember my life before having children, but I know for a fact it must have been horribly inconvenient without constantly having access to baby wipes. Now granted, before I had kids I probably had fewer messes to deal with every day, but let's face it, I was a bachelor. I wasn't exactly Mr. Clean. (Besides the fact that there is no possible way I could pull off the bald-with-a-gold-hoop-earring quasi pirate look, I wasn't all that clean either.) What did I use to clean up spills? Or shine my shoes? Or blow my nose, clean my sunglasses, dust the house, wash my hands, clean the dashboard, wash my feet, wipe down the kitchen, wash my face, check my oil, or polish the silverware? I probably just used my shirt like my kids do.

As if off-site bathrooms weren't enough of a concern, the bathrooms at home aren't exactly free from troubles either. Sure, the kids have easy access to them, but sometimes, that's the problem. Since we've had children, I have very rarely used my toilet by myself. Some little one either wants to come in to watch how it's done, or just needs to be in there with me to talk about what's going on. If I lock the door, that often leads to a lot of knocking, banging, or crying about not being able to get in.

Before I had kids I never gave one thought to the bathrooms at work. Now, I cherish them. Using the bathroom at work is the only time I ever have any privacy on the toilet anymore. I have resigned myself to the fact that I will have very little privacy in my own bathroom ever again, unless I can hold out until nine or ten o'clock at night when I'm relatively sure there won't be any more boys boomeranging out of bed to use the potty. But even after nine it's a crapshoot (so to speak). There is always the off chance that someone will still get up because "There's another poop in there," or "Whoops, I forgot to pee."

Go use the toilet at the park, kid. Here's some wipes.

Handy Parenting Tips
August 2, 2009

I have been a parent for a little while now, and along the way with my three boys I have picked up a few helpful hints that I would like to pass on to all you new parents out there, so here they are:

Smidge's Handy Tips and Helpful Advice for New Parents

Don't take the side of the bed closest to the door in your room. As soon as your children start getting out of bed in the middle of the night, you turn into the go-to parent for any and all late night activities. If your spouse won't switch sides with you, simply turn the bed around.

Once the kids start crawling and climbing, get rid of all of your chairs. It will just be easier that way.

Never say anything within a thousand yards of your children that you wouldn't want repeated in front of your in-laws or your pastor, because it will be.

Even if they have never been exposed to any kind of weapon, boys will naturally pick up a stick and pretend it's a gun, a sword, or a bludgeon. It's in their DNA.

Kids love to call other kids names. If your child is calling another kid a "stinky face," the best response is to immediately call your child a "poopy butt."

Up until the age of eighteen, when they can legally object, it is best to just put your kids back in diapers for long road trips. It's really the only way to make decent time.

Never ever give your children sugar under any circumstances.

74

If all of your kids are ever invited to the same sleepover, drop them off and immediately turn off your cell phones and go to Las Vegas for three days. They will be fine. They are in good hands, and it's really the only way you will ever get to go to Vegas.

A handy way to tire your kids out before bedtime is to have them drag your spare truck tire up and down the street on a rope until they fall over. When they hit the sidewalk, viola, ready for bed.

Purchase at least four to five times the amount of sippy cups that you think will be sufficient. Once a week, lift up all the furniture in the house and retrieve them. Wash with industrial caustic high-pressure foam or throw away as necessary.

A handy way to combat the garbage can flies that inevitably show up when disposable diapers are abundant is to light your trash can on fire every other day. This keeps the flies manageable and reduces the amount of garbage you are sending to the landfill. Win-win.

When at the zoo, never let your kids get into the monkey cage, no matter how much they beg. Just trust me.

If left unchecked, boys will attempt to pee anywhere on anything. Keep an eye on them at the mall!

It will end up being cheaper in the long run if you simply remove all the ceiling fans in your house and replace them with bullet-proof light fixtures. You can have ceiling fans again when they graduate from college.

Never ever wear the couple's matching shorts and shirt combos with the loud Hawaiian print. This has nothing to do with kids, it's just good common sense.

We have 32,000 pictures of our first boy, 46 pictures of our second boy, and no photographic evidence that we even have a third boy. Try to even out the photography if you can.

Ranch dressing, when left on a kid's face, produces a red rash. If done properly, it can end up looking like clown makeup that only lasts for about a half-hour.

And lastly, always keep a first aid kit handy. I imagine if you have girls, it should include Band-Aids and Neosporin. If you have boys it should also include a tourniquet, arm and leg splints, sutures, large butterfly bandages and gauze pads, local anesthetic, an immobilizing neck brace, saline IV bags, a defibrillator, a stretcher, and a fully-licensed paramedic.

I hope that was helpful for you. Good luck!

Insert Son A into House B
March 17, 2010

This weekend, my family had an impromptu picnic in our backyard to celebrate the return of the sun. As we lazed about on our blanket, my wife and I surveyed the hurricane debris-like spread of balls, Tonka trucks, scooters, bikes, baseball bats, mitts, and assorted plastic gardening equipment taking up approximately ninety percent of the back patio surface not already claimed by actual patio fixtures like tables and my giant manly stainless steel barbeque. We both decided it was time for some better outdoor storage for the boys' toys, so off to our local home improvement warehouse we went.

We scored a sweet clearance deal on two 130-gallon storage chests that are approximately two and a half feet wide by two and a half feet tall and five feet long. They have a nice flat lid, that when closed, becomes a handy bench seat. That is no less than sixty-two cubic feet of clean, dry, weatherproof storage that should leave us plenty of room to acquire the inevitable forty-five more cubic feet of toys in the coming years.

We tied those bad boys to the top of the Ford Expedition, and drove home triumphantly to begin the "easy assembly process."

When I cracked open the first of the two cardboard boxes, I found just what I was expecting. Six heavy-duty plastic sides, two metal hinge assemblies (complete with gas spring-assist shocks), one long metal reinforcing bar for the lid, and the assorted corner brackets and hardware to fasten everything together. Piece of cake.

The good folks at Suncast Outdoor Storage Products were also kind enough to include three copies of the owner's manual. One in English, and two in languages that I don't understand. I went with the English version.

One thing that separates me from many of the other males of the species is that I always read the instructions before I try to put anything together. It saves time and money. It also saves me from having to explain to the boys why some words are "adult words" that they're not allowed to use.

Almost immediately I became skeptical of the instructions when I read on the first page, "Only adults should set up the product. Do not allow children in the setup area until assembly is complete."

I thought to myself, "Uh-oh. The lawyers have gotten to them. There is no single part to this chest that weighs over seven pounds. How could a kid possibly get hurt during assembly? Besides, how will my boys learn anything if I don't at least let them watch?"

Then I lost all respect for the engineers at Suncast when I read, "Two adults required for this step" on the instructions of how to slide the two-pound side panel into its slots in the front and back panels. There is no way that I could need another adult to help me with this step. My kids could probably do it by themselves.

Even though I was totally disgusted with the instructions, I read to the end and then began the installation. I wasn't even half way through before I started to change my opinion of the guys that wrote the manual.

With my three young boys playing all around me on the back patio, I went to work. I had the base and all four sides on the chest in a matter of minutes. Just as I had suspected, the "need two adults" step took me about five seconds by myself. Ha! What were those manual writers thinking?

Almost as soon as I got the last side wall into position, the new toy chest began getting filled with toys. Balls, baseball bats, and plastic trucks were hurled at me from all directions, ricocheting around the inside of the chest and flying at my head. Progress was halted for a few minutes as I explained to the boys that they needed to wait until Daddy was done installing the lid before we could fill the chest.

The lid hinges were to be fastened to the side walls with screws. I had never given much thought to the individual parts list and count that you always find in manuals, detailing exactly how many #5-type screws you should have received. I always figured there was no sense spending time counting them. Either I had them or I didn't, and if I was short a screw or two, I would figure it out.

Well, I went to grab the eight #2-type screws I would need to fasten the hinges to the chest, and only two were sitting in the spot where I had left them on the patio table. One was on the ground under the table, and my two-year-old son was sitting a few feet away with three in his lap and one sticking out of his mouth. Two on the table, one on the ground, three from his lap and the one I just wrenched out of his mouth makes seven. I was supposed to have eight. Did he swallow one?!? Or did I even have eight to begin with? I never counted them!!

As I picked him up to inspect him for a perforated esophagus, the last #2 screw fell out of his pant cuff. Whew! That must be why they tell you how many you're supposed to have. Mental note to self: Always count them ahead of time to avoid unnecessary trips to the ER for exploratory hardware X-rays.

OK, crisis averted, and on to lid attachment. After I had retrieved the four #6-type screws from their new storage location on the ledge high above the sliding glass door, and out of reach of all two-year-olds, I was ready to fasten the long reinforcing bar into place. Now, where did that long reinforcing bar go? It was lying on the patio right in front of the new storage chest a minute ago. A yellow plastic Wiffle Ball bat has taken its place, but no reinforcing bar in sight.

After a lengthy interrogation of the four-year-old and the five-year-old, I was led to the fort that they had made with the cardboard lid of the shipping box. My five-foot-long reinforcing bar was stuck two feet into the mud, helping to support the fort's roof. I had to give them points for ingenuity and structural integrity, but I was not amused.

After cleaning off the bar on one of their shirts, I went back to work on the chest. While I was away dismantling the fort, the two-year-old had managed to put away a few more toys into the new chest. The reinforcing bar attaches to the inside of the lid, so I needed to step into the chest to do the work. No problem. I just scooted the soccer ball and Tonka truck out of the way with my foot, and stepped in. Thirty seconds later, the reinforcing bar was attached and the first of two new storage chests was completely assembled.

I stood up straight, stretched my back and swung my right leg out of the chest. Just before the weight transfer was complete I realized that I was about to step on the two-year-old, who had taken up a prone position in front of the new chest. I quickly and awkwardly adjusted the landing zone for my right foot, narrowly missing my youngest son, but planting my foot squarely on the yellow plastic Wiffle Ball bat.

I'm not one hundred percent sure what really happened next, but after some mid-air acrobatics, the end result was three young boys laughing hysterically, and me flat on my back inside my brand new Suncast Outdoor Storage Products 130-gallon storage chest with a soccer ball in my left kidney and my head resting rather uncomfortably on a Tonka truck.

As I lay there gazing up at the late afternoon sky, slipping in and out of consciousness, it occurred to me that the guys who wrote the instruction manual were some of the smartest men on the planet. They weren't lawyer-shy wimps or limp-wristed computer jockeys like I had first assumed. They were dads.

80

They advised me not to let the kids into the assembly area, and I didn't listen. Then they tried once more to keep me safe by suggesting that the project could not be completed without a second adult. It was my short-sighted machismo that kept me from seeing that warning for what it was. The second guy isn't there to help you with the assembly. He's there to keep a lookout for stray hardware and toys if you happened to ignore their first suggestion about no kids. He's also the guy that drives you to the hospital when you step on the Wiffle Ball bat.

I'm Finally That Guy
September 1, 2010

A big "Thank You" is going out to my youngest son this week. He has turned me into "That Guy." Allow me to explain.

It's really probably a common tale among parents. Before I had kids I would occasionally find myself at the mall or the grocery store, in awe of some poor parent whose kid was melting down. The child would be yelling, screaming, and throwing a fit, and there would be the parent, doing one of two things:

1) Threatening the kid with their very life as they dragged him out of the store.
2) Or, simply ignoring the kid and attempting to shop as if nothing was wrong.

Depending on the parent's reaction I always had either a feeling of pity for them, or a mixture of pity and mild disgust.

No matter what the circumstance though, I always had the thought in the back of my mind that, "My kids won't behave like that!"

Now, I am proud to report that at ages six, four and two, my boys have had very few public meltdowns. You will note I said, "very few," and not, "none." I have unfortunately been "that guy" a few times in the last six years, and it quickly dispelled my theory that my kids were perfect as well as my hope that I would never be seen leaving a Target dragging a screaming three-year-old behind me.

It is not bad behavior, however, that I am writing about today. No, I am writing today about another kind of inevitable kid situation that provokes sympathetic, empathetic, and sometimes just pathetic looks from the other parents in the near vicinity. With the kind of situation I am talking about, I have given

82

plenty of charitable "been there, buddy" looks to fellow dads, but last Wednesday, I really got a chance to be on the receiving end... big time.

I met my wife at the gym after work, where she was already splashing and playing with the three boys in the kids pool. Our gym has three pools; a kids pool with an adjacent water park, a lap pool, and a square, shallow, multi-purpose pool.

I had only been in and playing with the boys for about five minutes when the head lifeguard announced that everyone needed to get out of the kids pool and vacate the water park. He was sorry for the inconvenience, but we would need to remain out of the water for forty-five minutes. I asked my wife what was going on, and she said a little girl had thrown up in the pool, and they were required to chlorinate and skim before they could let everyone back in. The water park is fed with the water from the kids pool, so that needed to be shut down as well. No more fun! Everyone out!

Now, every parent knows there is no way to predict when a child might throw up. They are a lot like Coke bottles. Sometimes, they just blow. So, for the most part, I just shrugged my shoulders, and moved the kids out of the water. But somewhere in the back of my head, explicable only due to human nature, a little voice was saying, "Come on, dude! Why's your kid chunking in the pool? Thanks a lot, man. Now I have to go to the annoying pool."

The multi-purpose pool requires a much higher level of parental vigilance for us, because it has no gradual beach-entry shallow end like the kids pool. It starts at three feet deep, which is too deep for Son Number Three, so I need to hold him, or keep him corralled on the steps. Holding him wouldn't be so bad, as he is mostly calm and happy, but he is also intermittently scared to death of the water. It's a lot like holding a koala bear that occasionally turns into a crazed spider monkey. If you're not careful, he'll rip your nostrils right out!

We spent some time in the multi-purpose pool, nostril incident-free, and then got out to have our dinner. My wife had packed the boys some foil-wrapped bean burritos, and we all spread out on the warm concrete deck to eat. My wife left us there and headed home, and the boys and I ate and watched the ensuing aqua-aerobics class that had taken over the multi-purpose pool. After we had finished our burritos and I had answered approximately six thousand questions about aqua-aerobics, the lifeguard announced that the kids pool was back open for business.

Yay! Back to the kids pool for some more fun, and then home for bed. We hit the water with gusto, and were soon surrounded by twenty or thirty other frolicking kids and parents. Everyone was very happy to have the fun pool and water park back after the shutdown.

I was sitting in about two feet of water watching Son Number One and Two swimming with their goggles on, diving for toys. Son Number Three was behind me splashing water on my back, hollering and giggling. All was right with the world.

Then I noticed it.

At first I didn't know what to make of it. I thought someone had dropped some Cheerios or granola in the pool and it had started to disintegrate. The little brown particles were suddenly floating all around me, coming from somewhere behind me. Just about the time I started to turn around to investigate, one of the lifeguards shouted, "Hey, what's that?"

I turned around and sprang to my feet when I saw Son Number Three standing smack in the center of a brown, underwater particle cloud, radiating two to three feet in every direction. I snatched him up and did the stomach-over-the-forearm-pull-up-the-back-of-the-shorts poop check, and sure enough! Number Three had gone number two.

84

The kids pool had been re-opened for a grand total of four minutes and my boy had shut it down again!

Apparently, today's "swimmy diapers" can only do so much when you neglect to check them regularly.

One of the younger female lifeguards tried to make me feel better – probably after seeing the look of total disgust and shame on my face – by saying, "Don't worry. It happens all the time."

I just barely heard her, though, as I fireman-carried all three boys and our gear bag at a dead sprint toward the family bathroom.

The lifeguard hazmat response team was on the case, and I was not necessarily interested in staying poolside to preside over the evacuation and acknowledge the looks of scorn or pitiful understanding that I was sure to receive from the other parents.

It may "happen all the time," but I can assure you, when it's your turn to be "That Guy," you really don't want to hang around to take credit.

Cyclical Failure
November 17, 2010

I think if I had to boil down the essence of American fatherhood into one scene or activity, it would be the day out in the street when the father, running behind the child's bike, lets go of his grip on the back of the seat and watches proudly as his child rides a two-wheeler for the first time without the training wheels.

I could picture the scene in my mind. I would be sitting in my red leather chair in my study, wearing my crushed velvet smoking jacket and ascot, reading a classic novel. My son would knock respectfully at the door, and ask to speak to me about his bicycle. Having inherited my incredible balance and agility through his DNA, he would instinctively know he was ready to go from four wheels to two. He would beg me to remove the training wheels and I would ask him, "Are you sure you're ready?" in that really cool fatherly way, where I know he's ready, but I want to instill in him a sense of measured restraint and responsibility for his own actions, so I ask the question anyway in a concerned, caring, thoughtful, and deep voice.

He says, "Yes!" excitedly, because he knows all about my concerned, thoughtful voice, so he knows that I know that he knows that he's ready. I give him a wink. Without saying a word, the wink says, "You're turning out to be a fine lad, and you're making me proud." That one wink says it all. It's a wink he'll remember and cherish for the rest of his life.

We bound out to the garage where he sees that I have already removed his training wheels the day before, because I'm such an intuitive, thoughtful, caring dad that I can see these things coming. He smiles from ear to ear as he realizes how lucky he is to have me as his father. Out in the street, I run behind him

86

holding the back of the seat for a few minutes, and then, using my innate dad skills, I recognize the perfect time to let go, and he rides off on his own, in a glorious display of two-wheeled balance and agility. I stand in the middle of the street beaming with pride as the neighbors erupt in applause for my son's new achievement and for my superior dadliness.

That didn't happen.

For starters, I don't have a study, an ascot, or a son who knocks respectfully on anything, let alone a door. My wife and I have three boys, and crashing through doors head-first is about as restrained as they get. Anyway, my oldest son, Number One, as we refer to him, is about to turn six years old. I felt that it was about time he learned how to ride a two-wheeler, even though he had absolutely no interest in doing so. His younger brother, Number Two, is four and a half. He had plenty of interest in learning to ride a two-wheeler, but a distinct lack of balance, grace, agility, and good sense. He does have, however, a heaping helping of persistence.

I asked Number One to try.
He said, "No, thanks."
I told him we were going to take his training wheels off and give it a shot.
He cried.
A half-hour later I finally convinced him it would be a good idea, and he said, "OK."

I tried to hold his seat.
He fell over.
I tried to hold his shoulders.
He fell over.
I tried to hold the handle bars.
He ran over my foot. Then he fell over.
He said he was finished.
I said, "OK."

I limped back to the garage.

Number Two announced that he was ready to give it a spin.

I iced my foot.

He begged.

I said, "Maybe later."

He pleaded.

I said, "OK."

I took the training wheels off of Number Two's bike and out to the street we went.

I tried to hold his seat.

He fell over.

I tried to hold his shoulders.

He fell over.

I tried to hold the handle bars.

We ran into a parked car.

He asked me to stop helping him.

Number One looked at me and said, "Dad, you're really bad at that. You dropped me every time, and you ran him into a car."

I had no argument in my favor. Now, in my defense, they were completely leaning to one side, not pedaling, not steering, not helping in any way, but the end result was, in fact, that I had ran Number Two into a car. The results speak for themselves.

I gave up and went inside. Son Number One went back to playing tether ball, but Number Two was not to be deterred. He decided that if his dad couldn't help him, he would just have to figure it out on his own. For the next three days, at every opportunity he had, he was out on his bike without training wheels, trying to learn to ride. Occasionally I would offer helpful advice, and he would give me a perfunctory, "OK, Daddy," that really meant, "I'll take it from here, old man. You may go now."

When I returned home from work on the fourth day, I was greeted by a positively beaming Number Two, who was tearing up and down the street on two wheels. He had done it. And, he had done it all by himself! I found myself more proud of him than if I had helped. He had overcome the giant hurdle of a useless coach and won the game on his own. He was truly an all-star.

He was also very, very aware of the fact that he could now ride a two-wheeler and his older brother couldn't. He was so aware of that situation that I began to question his true motives. Had he done it so that he could accomplish a personal goal, or had he done it to stick it in his brother's face? Hmmm.

The answer began to clear up at dinner that night. Our boys know that bragging is forbidden at our house, but, if you don't mind me saying, they're smarter than average in my opinion. My four-and-a-half-year-old knows that stating facts is not necessarily forbidden, so he decided to make some observations.

"Hey, Dad."
"Yes?"
"I'm four and a half."
"Yep."
"Did you like how I rode my two-wheeler today?"
"Yes I did. I was very impressed."
"Hey, Dad."
"Yes?"
"He's almost six."
"I know that."
"I like riding my two-wheeler."
"That's enough."
"What?!?"

Can you guess who asked me to remove his training wheels again that night? Two days later, Son Number One was back on top, no longer the kid whose younger brother could out-ride him.

I set out to teach my boys how to ride a bike. Four days later they had learned absolutely nothing from me, but I had learned a valuable lesson from them. Sibling rivalry is going to be a wonderful tool for me. It's way more effective than anything I can say. Number Three doesn't stand a chance!

As Son Number Two zoomed up to me that evening on his super-cool green motocross bike, I gave him the knowing wink. That one wink that says it all.

He just stared at me blankly. Oh, well.

The Tooth Fairy
January 19, 2011

It is really starting to amaze me what kids will believe. I mean, we just got through Christmas and the whole Santa Claus thing again. Here's the story, kid: A fat man in a red suit who lives at the top of the world with a bunch of toy-making elves came to our house in a sleigh pulled by flying deer. He landed on our roof and came down our chimney while we were all sleeping and delivered Razor scooters.

Now, never mind the logistics of a round-the-world trip with six billion stops in one night. That is the easiest part of the story to swallow as far as I'm concerned. We have a concrete tile roof with no snow and a thirty-five-degree pitch, yet my kids think someone landed a sleigh on it. Apparently, flying deer make sense to them, and the fact that our gas fireplace chimney is really just a 3-inch diameter pipe doesn't faze them. I guess they figure if the fat man can get here with flying deer, he can fit himself, two Razor scooters and a soccer ball down a hole the size of a water glass.

I have to cut them some amount of slack regarding Santa, since it's undoubtedly the most popular world-wide myth being perpetrated on children. It's easier to fool them because we parents have our story straight about Saint Nick.

We are currently dealing with another benevolent, magical house-visiting stranger, but this one is weirder. Weirder than a man who lives with scooter-producing elves and flying caribou, you ask? Yes. I'm talking about the Tooth Fairy.

My six-year-old, Son Number One as he is called, has been losing his baby teeth for a while now. He recently lost number three and four, which happened to be his two front teeth, so he now looks like a really unfortunate beaver. When he lost his first tooth about a year ago, we introduced the Tooth Fairy to the boys.

Here's how the conversation went:
"Now that you've lost this tooth, we need to put it in an envelope and put it under your pillow."
"Why"
"So the Tooth Fairy will come and bring you money."
"The Tooth Fairy?"
"Yes. The Tooth Fairy comes and takes your teeth out from under your pillow and leaves you money."
"Oh, OK."

OK?!? What do you mean, "OK?" Don't you have about a bazillion other questions?

Who is the Tooth Fairy? Is the Tooth Fairy a he or a she? Where does she live? How does she know where we live? How does she get in the house? How does she get into our room? How does she know which room is ours? How does she get under my pillow? Why do we leave the tooth under my pillow instead of out on the dresser? How does she even know I lost a tooth? There are three of us in this room, so how does she know which pillow? Does she just check under all the pillows? Why does this happen at night instead of at lunch or at school?

And the biggest unasked question, in my opinion…"WHY?" Why does the Tooth Fairy want my teeth? Why is she willing to pay for them? What does she do with them?

I mean, as an adult, I would immediately question her motives as well as her under-the-pillow drop spot. Santa can do his thing downstairs by the fireplace all night as far as I'm concerned, but if you're telling me someone will be getting under my pillow while I'm sleeping on it, some serious questions are going to be asked. And if I don't like any of the answers, the Tooth Fairy is likely to find a gun under that pillow, not an incisor.

But, a simple, "OK," is what I got from my boys, and they woke up in the morning excited about Son Number One's shiny new dollar coin. They are really gullible! That reminds me… We parents really need to get on the same page about a few things regarding this tooth-hoarding nymph.

For starters, we should all come to a consensus on amount of money given per tooth. Back in my day it was a nickel or a dime at my house, but some of the kids at school were getting quarters. I always thought that was a little weird. Why did she pay Billy more for his stupid teeth?

Nowadays, with the inflated price of health care, we're up to a dollar per tooth with my kids, but I have heard some parents saying five dollars. Besides the fact that I have three boys and would go broke at five dollars per tooth, it just seems like too much. At those prices the kids might start getting suspicious and asking more questions, and I think we can all agree that nobody wants that. Also, if the price gets too high, we'll have kids in the garage pulling out each other's teeth with dad's needle-nose pliers, trying to score enough cash for a new Nintendo. Not good.

We also need to agree on what she does with the teeth. We should get our story straight for the kids, but mostly we should all figure out what to actually do with the teeth. My wife and I are currently saving them in an envelope, but neither one of us can figure out who's idea that was, or why we're doing it. What are we saving them for?

Come to think of it, I'm out four bucks so far, and all I have to show for it is four used teeth that I don't really want in an envelope. Maybe my boys aren't the gullible ones in this situation.

Why ARE we keeping these? Why are we paying our children for their old teeth? Those are really the big unanswered questions here. I have four tiny teeth in my dresser drawer that I don't want right now, and I would really like to get those questions answered before I'm down sixty bucks, holding sixty baby teeth, and wondering, "What now?"

Let's all get together and discuss. I can meet on Thursday evenings.

Potty Training Out Loud
May 11, 2011

Son Number Three just turned three years old and is the last one in diapers. We started potty training him last week. I don't know if you have ever potty trained anyone or anything, but let me tell you, it can get exciting for a whole bunch of different reasons.

For starters, my wife and I are excited at the prospect of being done with diapers for good. We've been knee-deep in them for six and a half years now, and we can finally see the light at the end of the dark and stinky tunnel. It's such a wonderful thought that we almost dare not speak it, for fear of jinxing it.

No more expensive diapers! No more expensive wipes. No more disgusting diapers! No more used wipes. No more storing used diapers and their nefarious contents in my garage. No more storing eight-foot-square Costco-sized cases of diapers in my garage. No more packages of diapers and wipes falling out at me from every closet in the house.

No more questioning Son Number Three about the current situation in his pants. No more needing to check the validity of said boy's answer. (He has never been very reliable.) Never again will we need to bend down and go sniffing around his butt like an ill-mannered hound dog. No more stomach-over-the-forearm, pull-up-the-back-of-the-shorts visual poop checks. We are mere days away from becoming a civilized family that fully utilizes their indoor plumbing. It's all very exciting!

Then there is the other kind of excitement. Part of the deal with potty training involves gambling. This is when you put the child in "big boy underwear" and let them roam freely around the house, while you chew your nails and inquire with them every ten to twelve seconds if they need to go sit on the potty. About every half-hour or so, your nerves are so frayed that you just go set them on the potty as a preemptive measure.

At our house, if you pee on the potty, you get five M&Ms. For our kids who don't get candy on a regular basis, that tends to be a big deal. If you poop on the potty, you get a whole bunch of M&Ms. The amount varies depending on how excited the parent is that they just dodged a bullet. I give him the whole bag.

Most of the time, however, you end up cleaning up a mess instead of handing out congratulatory candy-coated chocolate. With Son Number Three, this has been quite an ordeal. Not due to the messes so much as the raw emotion involved. You see, Number Three is either not very smart, or a super-genius. I haven't decided which yet. He either can't seem to get his terminology right, or he is so brilliant that at age three, he has already mastered reverse psychology and corporate-level negotiating techniques. Allow me to explain.

He keeps mixing up the terms "poop" and "pee." He will be in big boy underwear upstairs and yell down in a sad voice that he is poopy. You run upstairs in a panic, expecting the worst, only to find that he has peed, but not pooped.

Because you were mentally prepared for the worst, after you realize the real situation at hand, you are actually happy to only be cleaning up pee. You are so happy not to be scrubbing something far worse out of the upholstery that you almost thank him for peeing in his pants and on the couch. Go figure.

Like I said, he may be the smartest kid on the planet, or he may just be really bad with terminology. I'm leaning toward the latter, because I can't really see any upside to peeing all over yourself and missing out on free candy, and a genius would have probably figured that out by now, three years old or not.

Anyway, we're in the midst of it all, and we're excited that we're so close to being diaperless. My wife is so excited about the prospect of a carefree life without poopy pants that she temporarily lost her mind the other day, and inadvertently gave me the opportunity to discover just how excited I really am about living a diaper-free life.

I was at the office and my cell phone rang. It was my wife, who in an excited voice announced that Number Three had just pooped on the potty, and then immediately put Number Three on the phone. She didn't ask me where I was or if I could talk, she just put him on the phone. Then, my three-year-old tells me he just pooped on the potty, FOR THE VERY FIRST TIME IN HIS WHOLE LIFE.

I am standing in the middle of my office. My co-workers are all around, and my son is breathlessly awaiting my response. I need to make a very quick decision. On the one hand, I obviously need to be very excited and congratulatory. This is a huge deal and needs to be treated that way. We need to joyously convey the message to him that we are very happy and he has done a great thing.

On the other hand, I am at the office, and would like to maintain a certain level of decorum. I am standing next to the boss's office. There are people on the phone with customers. On the whole, I would like to keep things with my colleagues on a professional level, and joyous congratulations about pooping aren't exactly professional.

I learned something about myself that day. I realized, almost instantly, that my distain for dirty diapers greatly outweighs my desire to remain professional.

"GREAT JOB POOPING ON THE POTTY, BUDDY!" I yelled into the phone.

Work is a little weird now, but I don't care. I really want to be done with diapers!

No Respect
May 18, 2011

I'm starting to feel like my wife. At least, how I think she must feel, when she's dealing with our kids. She gets no respect.

Now, let's be clear. She *does* get the kind of respect that is required of children by their parents. For the most part they come when called and do what they are asked. Some days they are on the ball, and some days they give her just enough respect in the right areas to avoid physical harm, but on the whole, they behave themselves for her. It's in the area of knowledge and opinion that she gets the short end of the stick. They will not take her word for anything, but they will believe anything I tell them.

Neither of us knows why that is, but it has been the case for as long as we can remember. At least it had until a few days ago. Apparently, God is finally feeling sorry for my wife, and has sent our third child, Son Number Three, to set things straight.

The turning point occurred the other day when my three-year-old son sat down on the floor to put his flip-flops on. He gets one on his foot, looks up at me, and asks, "Is this the right foot?" I tell him no… and he argues with me.

Excuse me? I am your father. I know which foot is which, and which shoe goes on which foot, thank you very much!

"No, Son, that is not the right foot."
"Yes it is."

(Not only was it the wrong flip-flop for the chosen foot, but it was also his left foot, so there was no way I was misinterpreting his question. He was just flat-out wrong.)

"No it isn't. That one goes on the other foot."

"Mommy!"

"You don't need to ask Mommy. I know which is which."

"No you don't. Mommy!"

"I assure you, I know all about shoes and feet. We don't need to consult Mommy."

"Mommy!"

I was dumbfounded. Not only was my three-year-old ignoring my shoe advice, but he was blatantly telling me I didn't know what I was talking about. We were in brand new territory for me here. Up until this point, my knowledge and opinion on any subject had stood without question. Not with my wife, mind you, or any other adult for that matter, but with my kids.

With the first two, I could tell them anything and they would believe me. I told them Jell-O was made out of cow bones, and they just said, "Cool." If their mom told them that the sky was blue, they would run and check with me. (Both of those things are true, but which one would you question?)

When Mommy showed up to help out with the shoe debate, I was forced to stand there and listen while my wife explained to our third child that daddy knows how shoes work, just like she does, and it's OK to listen to me about which foot is which. Then she stood up, and with a wry smile, gave me a consoling kiss on the cheek, and a not-so-consoling giggle.

Later that day, my wife was going to be gone for a few hours at dinner time. She cooked us a pizza before she left, kissed the boys, and headed out the door. Five minutes later, I told the boys it was time for dinner. Son Number One and Two headed for the table, but Number Three argued with me.

"No! Mommy said it wasn't dinner time yet. Mommy said we have to wait. Mommy said her chart sayed below for drain." (Sometimes he's pretty hard to understand, especially when he's worked up.) I actually had to pick him up to keep him from

100

trying to drag me out of the kitchen, calm him down, and show him the cooked pizza before he would believe me.

Now, I guess it wouldn't be so bad if I thought that Son Number Three just didn't trust my opinion on certain subjects. It would be weird, but it would at least be semi-tolerable. The problem is, I'm getting the feeling he doesn't think I have any authority in any matters. I have received some pretty clear evidence that this is the case in the last few days.

We have a rule in our house. No answer shopping. If you don't like daddy's answer to your question of, "May I go play with this real sword I just found," you are not allowed to go ask your mother the same question in hopes of a better answer. (That's actually a bad example, because I would have probably said, "Yes.") Anyway, the rule is, you take the answer you get and don't go looking for a better one somewhere else.

Son Number Three is apparently so off the rails with his lack of trust in my ability to parent him that he has actually started reverse answer shopping. Here is an actual conversation I had with him the other day:

"Daddy, can I have a cookie?"
"Yes."
"Mommy! Can I have a cookie?"

I mean, seriously! What kind of logic is that? Is he honestly thinking, "Well, OK. This man here just gave me the answer I was looking for, but I'm not confident that he has my best interests at heart. I'm not sure that I trust his judgment, and as such, even though I really want that delicious cookie, I think I will consult an adult that I know loves and cares for me."

This newfound situation has me thrown for a loop. My wife thinks it is endlessly humorous, but I am at a loss. Why doesn't my third child trust me? What have I done to bring this on?

Maybe... just maybe, like his mom, he doesn't think that kids should play with real swords?

Nah! That can't be it.

The Great Juice Caper
October 5, 2011

Son Number Two is five years old and is almost two months into his first year of kindergarten. (We are hoping it's his first and only year of kindergarten, but based on our experience, you never can tell.) He has a best buddy in his class named Luke, and he and Luke are as thick as thieves. Actually, they are thieves.

Now, it is no surprise when little kids get into mischief. What is surprising is when two five-year-olds get together, hatch a devious and complicated plan involving simultaneous stealth and deception in two separate houses, and execute the plan flawlessly every day for two weeks unbeknownst to their parents, only getting caught by sheer happenstance.

The silent alarm that these two miniature partners in crime unknowingly tripped came in the form of a casual conversation between a mother and a teacher. My wife was volunteering in Number Two's classroom one morning, and had a few spare minutes to chat with Mrs. Camarda.

"Your son is a real pleasure to have in this class."
"Thank you."
"He is such a sweet boy. He and Luke are inseparable. They are so cute at lunch with their juice."
"Excuse me?"
"I said he is a sweet boy…"
"No, no. About the juice."
"Oh, you know. When he and Luke buy their juices at lunch. They think that is so fun."
"He buys juice at lunch!?!"
"Well, not every day. Sometimes they buy chocolate milk."
"What!?!"

Upon further questioning, it turns out that the cafeteria at my son's elementary school sells juice for a quarter and chocolate milk for fifty cents. Number Two and his buddy had been throwing back delicious lunch-time school beverages every day for at least two weeks. Luke's mom happened to be volunteering on the same day, so she was immediately brought into the conversation to compare notes. Both boys were being sent to school each day with a lunch box and a bottle of water, and neither one had ever been authorized by a parent to purchase any extracurricular liquids, nor was either one ever given any money to do so.

My wife called me later that morning in hysterics. Hysterical laughing, that is. She explained what she had learned, and amazed, noted that Number Two had somehow apparently been leaving the house with money in his pocket every morning without us knowing. The questions were plentiful. Where was he getting the money? When was he getting it? Was he bringing money for Luke, also, or vice versa? Why is juice only a quarter? Can I, as a dad, get in on that? Etc.

As any good parents would do, we weighed our response options. How should we handle this? Should we sit him down and have a talk with him, or booby trap his piggy bank and scare the living daylights out of him? We debated for a while, but in the end, our hand was forced by the sheer lack of information we had. The junior juice larcenists had us in the dark. We had no idea where the money was coming from, so we were forced to talk with him without setting any elaborate trip wire/air horn devices. Oh, well.

Aside from being a key player in a beverage crime syndicate, Son Number Two is generally a very honest and generous boy. We were sure of a few things: If he was getting the money from a piggy bank, it would be from his own. (His older brother, Son Number One, would have been a whole different story.) Also, it was possible that he was funding the whole operation. He would happily buy his friend juice every day without thinking

104

twice about it, and that would put us in the awkward position of needing to praise his generosity while chastising his deception.

As it turned out, each member of the Capri Sun cartel was paying his own way. Upon intense questioning by two moms who were trying very hard not to laugh, both boys sang like canaries. With an odd mix of relief and disappointment, my wife found out that Luke was the mastermind. It was his idea to steal the car, and our son had decided to come along for the joy ride. Number Two had been sneaking downstairs to his piggy bank early each morning to get his daily quarter and secret it into the pocket of his school clothes before getting dressed. As it turned out, Luke didn't have access to his piggy bank, so he had been swiping coins from him mom's kitchen change jar that was meant for vacation spending money. Busted!

They were getting together each day to decide on juice or chocolate milk, so they would know if tomorrow would be a one or two-quarter day. That is seriously long-range planning for five-year-olds, and amazing when you compare it to their lack of ability to remember almost anything else about their daily routine. Number Two can't remember to brush his teeth even though he has to do it every morning and evening. He can't remember to wash his hands even though he has to do it before every meal. But when it comes to deception and covert refreshment operations, he can remember to hold daily planning meetings, remember what the next day's cash requirements are, and remember to pilfer the correct amount each morning before dawn. Go figure.

When all the details of the caper were uncovered, the four parents had a good chuckle, but our reactions to the miniature crime spree were mixed. We all had the same general thought, but the men and women viewed it from slightly different sides, as is so often the case.

Both mothers said, "Oh, great. They're able to fool us already, and they're only five years old. High school is going to be a disaster!"

Both dads said, "Holy cow. They can already fool us at five years old. That is so cool. I wonder what kind of stuff they're going to be able to pull off by the time they're in high school?"

Women are always looking at things so backward.

6

The Spica Cast

Nothing can prepare you for your three-year-old becoming luggage.

The "Free" Play Structure
October 12, 2011

I now have a huge, redwood play structure in my backyard. It takes up one whole side of my back lawn. It has a big elevated deck with a sloping roof, two regular swings, a rope swing, a weird ball and handle swing, a chain ladder, a rope ladder, a regular ladder, and a slide. It even has an extra tire swing, if I could figure out where to mount it. The kids love it. Well, two out of the three love it, anyway.

We just got it this weekend. It was free. At least, my wife says it was free. I look at that a little differently. The price we paid for it was definitely zero dollars, as it was given to us by a friend of a friend whose family had outgrown it. The costs associated with getting this backyard behemoth to our house are another matter.

As my wife raves about our new "free" play structure, I just can't help adding a few things up in my head:

Let's see...

There were the three cases of beer that I bought for our friend and the previous owner as a thank-you. That was $49.

There was the twenty-four-foot U-Haul truck that I had to rent to move the play structure from three towns away. That was $97.

There was gas for the U-Haul truck. That was $33.

There was the beer I bought for my brother-in-law and my friend who came over to help me retrieve, transport, and re-assemble the play structure. That was $32.

And lunch for the crew. One of whom ate three Chipotle burritos. $40.

And a pizza dinner for the crew and their families, since reassembly of the gargantuan play structure took all afternoon. Another $45.

If my math is correct, that already makes our free play structure cost at least $296. But let us not forget the hidden costs. I will inevitably have future work day obligations at my brother-in-law's house and my friends' houses to properly complete the cycle of home improvement assistance reciprocation. Not only do those future days have gas and travel costs associated with them, but opportunity costs associated with all the things I won't otherwise get done that day. Also, I'm confident that my wife will want to get rid of the grass that is currently under the new play structure, and replace it with decorative bark. There's another future weekend down the drain, and bark is not exactly free.

And as for this past weekend, we also need to take into consideration the gas my wife and I used to get the U-Haul and the meals. The gas my crew used to get to my house and back. The thirteen wood screws and two lag bolts that I had to find in my garage to finish the installation. All these things add up.

108

Then, there's also the ER bills. And the cost of the overnight hospital stay. The bill for the team of two orthopedic surgeons and the anesthesiologist in the OR. The missed day of work I had while getting the three-year-old's femur re-set in a cast. Those things might add up.

Did I forget to mention the broken leg?

Now, Son Number Three has been to the park probably hundreds of times. He has played on countless different sizes of play structures, both at parks, school playgrounds, and other people's houses. He has never jumped off the top of any of those.

Apparently, however, when the play structure is suddenly located in your very own backyard, that obviously means that you can also fly. At least, to my three-year-old it did. Ten minutes after we finished the installation, that play structure got a whole lot less free when mini Superman learned a hard lesson about gravity versus imaginary superpowers.

I haven't received any bills from the hospital yet, but after going back through my records on some of our previous ER visits and hospital stays, I'm estimating the "free" play structure is going to end up costing me about $27,000, give or take a few hundred bucks.

Outstanding. Oh, well. At least I have less lawn to mow now.

The Spica Cast
October 19, 2011

"Daddy, I need to pee."

"OK, buddy, hang on. I'll be right there."

My fully potty trained, three-year-old son is lounging on his back in the corner of the living room in a borrowed bean bag chair. He cannot be bothered to get up. I grab the plastic urinal bottle out of the "potty bucket," and get down on my knees in front of him. I undo the protective outer size-6 diaper, and pull the inner size-4 diaper from its tucked-in position. I slide the plastic urinal between the bean bag and the wooden dowel, get it into position, and tell him to go for it.

Suddenly, everything is going wrong. Pee is spraying everywhere. I frantically try to reposition the bottle, but the pee just keeps going everywhere except where it is supposed to. What is happening? Why is this not working? Why am I an idiot? I left the cap on the urinal bottle. I think we're going to have to keep this bean bag chair.

Such is life with a groggy dad and three-year-old in a Spica cast.

Son Number Three broke his femur last weekend, and we are in the middle of week two of the Spica cast. In case you are like me and had never heard of a Spica cast before, SPICA stands for Sadistic Physician's Inconvenient Children's Apparatus. At least, I think that's what it stands for. They didn't actually tell us.

Since they cannot do orthopedic surgery on small children, apparently, the only way to mend a broken thigh bone in a three-year-old is to put him in the cast equivalent of a lower-body straight jacket. He is armor plated and immobile from his

110

chest all the way down to his toes on the bad leg, and to mid-thigh on the good leg, with a nifty wooden dowel spreader bar attached at an angle between the two legs to keep them apart and rigid.

Our once highly mobile little boy is now basically luggage. He stays where we put him until it's time to pick him up and move him again. Unlike a suitcase, however, his seemingly super-convenient wooden handle is strictly off limits for lifting. Plus, he yells when he gets bored. My Samsonite never does that.

Our orthopedic surgeon told us, about the cast, "If we ever come up with a better way to do this, we will. But as of right now, this is as good as it gets."

As we were getting the tutorial on how to kinda sorta stuff a diaper up in and around the poop and pee access hatch, and then kinda sorta keep it in place with a bigger diaper around the outside of the cast, and then just sorta try to keep everything as clean as possible for the next four to five weeks, I thought to myself, "We put a man on the moon, but this is the best we as a country have to offer in the area of preschooler bone mending? I don't think we've really fully applied ourselves here."

I guess I could put my engineering brain to work and try to come up with something more convenient, but it will have to wait. As the urinal bottle incident attests, I am not getting a whole lot of sleep lately. Just when my wife and I thought we were done with the sleepless nights of infant care and feeding, we're suddenly back to sleeping in shifts. And the sleep we are getting is the non-satisfying light sleep that new parents and soldiers know all too well. Deep sleep never comes when your brain is busy listening for something all night.

We should be back to normal sleep in a few days. His pain level seems to be dropping off steadily, and he's becoming his old cheery self during the days, albeit a little more hyper at times.

We can't fault him for that, though. When you cage a wild monkey, you'd better expect to hear the bars rattle.

On the first night that we were back from the hospital, I told him I was going to carry him up to his room, to which he replied, "Daddy, I don't want to wear my cast to bed." He has since grasped the concept a little better, and has accepted his new reality a lot better than we thought he would. He even has a pretty good handle on the maintenance issues. His grandma and grandpa are here helping out, and the other night he announced that he had accidentally pooped in his diaper, instead of waiting for the bed pan. His grandma was the only one in the room when he made the announcement, and he looked at her concerned expression and asked, "Grandma, do you know how to do this?" When she hesitated, he said, "Go get Mommy, please."

We can't really leave him in the care of anyone not prepared to handle the Spica cast, which is pretty much everyone else, so his social calendar has been put on hold. He is playing hooky from preschool for the next month, and my wife's daily gym visits have stopped abruptly. The good news on both those counts is that he is no doubt being read to more now than ever before, and his cast weighs as much as he does, so my wife is probably getting a better weightlifting workout at home.

You have to look on the bright side of things in this life. Our precious little baby boy is hurting, but we've received more casseroles and cookies in the last week than you can shake a stick at. Some clouds have a delicious, buttery, oven-baked lining.

The Spica Cast, Part II
October 26, 2011

My three-year-old smells horrible. The boy reeks. He smells so bad, he's hard to love. We are a little over two weeks into our Spica cast adventure, and it's getting hard to take.

As it turns out, the Spica cast on a preschooler has a few hidden logistical issues. For starters, the only parts of him that are not in the cast are half a leg, some shoulders, arms and a head. That means that almost eighty to ninety percent of his skin is under the cast. Anyone who has ever worn a cast on any amount of their skin will attest to that being a major problem from the sweat/itch/stink "trifecta of fun" standpoint.

Now, for the mostly potty-trained preschool crowd, add wet diapers to the mix, and you've got yourself one smelly party.

During the day, pee is not an issue (as long as the parent running the urinal bottle has their head in the game). At night, however, the diaper occasionally gets peed in during a deep sleep. If all parties involved are sleeping, that diaper can stay wet and tucked inside that cast for hours.

Mind you, the diaper is doing its job. The people at Huggies have got super-absorbency down to a science. There are no liquids getting into the cast. But keep that wet diaper tucked inside a hot, sweaty cast for a while, and the vapors tend to migrate up into the cast lining. The result is a three-year-old with such a pungent ammonia smell about him that if you get within three feet of him, your eyes water.

We, as his family, have the ability to get away from him if we need to. He is trapped, however, with his nose six inches from the top of the cast. If he comes through this with any sense of smell left at all, it will be a miracle.

During many of the daytime hours, my youngest son can be found lying on his stomach on top of his beanbag chair, sans diaper, proudly airing out his butt. It's not dignified, but it is necessary. Besides, he's three, so he could care less.

There's one other reason I'm really glad he's only three and doesn't have a developed sense of dignity or shame. That would be the Summer's Eve feminine deodorant spray. My wife has been scouring the internet, reading Spica cast tips from parents who have gone through this, and feminine deodorant spray was one of the suggestions to combat the stink.

I read the directions printed on the back of the flowery pink and white aerosol spray can: "Shake well; remove cap. Hold can eight to twelve inches away from your lovely lady parts, and spray away."

I'm so glad he probably won't remember this.

After watching my wife spraying the exact opposite parts intended for use with said deodorant, and getting a whiff of the now flowery smelling ammonia cloud, I decided a more manly approach was required. Something with 110 volts. Something with some serious power. Something with spinning rotor blades and pressure differentials. We needed air flow, people. We didn't need to cover up the smell, we needed to blow it away!

I set out into my garage to make a ventilator for the boy. We would be cooling him off and airing him out in no time.

Prototype Number One involved a twenty-inch box fan, like the kind you use to ventilate a whole room. I fashioned a giant pyramid-shaped funnel out of cardboard and a half a roll of duct tape that necked the twenty-inch square fan housing down to a three-inch hole. My plan was to duct tape a vacuum cleaner hose to the hole, with the crevice tool attachment on the end of the hose. We could then stick the crevice tool down his cast, fire up the fan, and de-stink-ify our patient.

The only problem with the final product was that it was really big. It was lightweight and had a convenient handle, but the whole thing ended up being the size of a small filing cabinet. Just prior to attaching the hose, I happened to be in our bathroom and noticed - perhaps for the first time in my whole life - that my wife's hairdryer had a "cool" button.

I charged downstairs and confronted her. "Your hairdryer has a cool button!"
"Yeah, so what?"
"Why didn't you tell me?"
"All hairdryers have a cool button. Why would I have told you that?"
"They do?"
"Yes, moron. How is the house-sized ventilator fan coming?"

Prototype Number Two involved a ten-dollar hairdryer, and the vacuum attachments I was going to use on Prototype Number One. It was a lot easier to make, and only took me about ten minutes to put together. I proudly displayed the new anti-stink solution to the family.

"What happened to the giant, inconvenient fan?"
"I ended up going a different direction. Say hello to the hand-held model."

With the cool button locked down, I fired up the Conair Cast Savior 2000 and felt the perfectly cool air rush out of the crevice tool and across my face. Oh, the joy. Oh the ventilating that would soon… wait a minute. The cool air was suddenly not so cool. In fact, it was warm and getting warmer. As it turns out, hairdryers were not meant to force air through three feet of flexible vacuum hose and a skinny nozzle. The motor couldn't handle the pressure it was being asked to produce, and subsequently began heating up. Forcing hot air down an already warm cast seemed like a pretty bad idea. Starting an electrical fire near an immobile three-year-old didn't sound like such a great idea either, so I was back to the drawing board.

"What's wrong, honey? The 'cool button' not working out for you?"
"I just need to make some minor adjustments, that's all."

After my walk of shame back to the garage, the first adjustment I made was removing the hose from the hairdryer, and throwing the hairdryer in the garbage can. Now all I needed to do was figure out what to attach the hose to. Would my pride let me go back to the box fan? Would my wife ever let me live that down? Probably not, but it would be worth it if we could get rid of the ammonia smell... Suddenly, it hit me. The Aerobed!

Of course! Why didn't I think of this before? Our inflatable Aerobed portable mattress has a big, beefy air blower on it. That thing is so powerful you can lie on the mattress while you're filling it up. That baby will surely do the trick. I ran upstairs to the hall closet, yanked it off the shelf, brought it back to the garage, and pulled it out of its carrying case. All I have to do is take the motor and blower off the mattress and then... Oh, darn...

Can I really justify this? I could always go back to the box fan... But this would work so well. He really, really stinks. She'll probably understand...

Ten minutes later I walked back into the house holding Prototype Number Three. The coffee can-sized black blower motor was skillfully attached to the vacuum hose with enough duct tape to adequately cover up the ragged edges of blue mattress vinyl that I had to cut with my razor blade knife to free the molded-on pump housing from the mattress itself. For good measure, I used enough silver tape to cover up the Aerobed logo on the motor.

As I opened my mouth to tell the world of my triumph, my wife called to me from the kitchen. "Come here, honey. Look what I found online. It's called the CastCooler. You just wrap it around the cast, hook up your vacuum cleaner's hose to it, turn on the vacuum, and it pulls fresh air into the cast and removes all the moisture and stink. I just bought one on Amazon for $39.99."

"Wow. Sounds great, sweetheart. That should really do the trick."
"Did you want to show me something?"
"No. I'm just going to head back to the garage."

I need to go get rid of a queen-sized blue tarp with the giant hole in it and order a new Aerobed.

The Spica Cast, Part III
November 2, 2011

I abandoned my principles on Monday, along with my scruples, my dignity and my pride. On Monday evening I went from solid, upstanding dad, to lowlife, begging, loser. It was really quite pathetic, but totally worth it.

As you probably know, my youngest son is in his fourth week of being confined to a Spica cast in order to heal his broken femur. He is dealing with being confined to his cast far better than his mommy is dealing with being confined to the house with him, but that is a whole other topic, and one I can't really get into with you, for fear that she might kill me. Seriously, she's that stir-crazy. Anyway…

All three boys were planning to be matching ninjas this Halloween. They already had their costumes, but when Son Number Three broke his leg and ended up in the mother of all casts, we talked pretty seriously about just getting four feet of gauze and covering up what was left of his skin, and going with "mummy-boy."

He wasn't having any of it. He politely explained to his mother that he would be a ninja, just like we had planned, because that was what he wanted to be, and also, "Mummies can't pee." We couldn't fight our way through that iron-clad logic, so ninja it was.

Despite being completely rigid from the armpits down, he actually still fits in our stroller. We had already sold or donated our entire armada of strollers except one, which I had been constantly tripping over and cursing in my garage. I happily pulled it out of retirement when we realized he could "sit" right on the front edge. His cast is too wide for him to go all the way back into the seat, but if we stuff two bed pillows behind him he

118

can kind of recline at a thirty-degree angle with his leg sticking straight out in front, like a fiberglass battering ram. Cross your fingers that the miniature plastic stroller seat belt holds tight, and presto, movable child.

On the big night, my wife basically just sort of tied his black and red polyester ninja outfit to his cast. He was able to wear the torso portion and the ninja hood, but the legs of the costume were only able to lie on top of his legs. Fortunately, the costume came with ninja leg tie straps that I assume were supposed to simulate some kind of really inconvenient ancient Japanese footwear. On a normal five and six-year-old boy, they stay tied to their calves for about two minutes, then drag on the ground tripping the so-called ninja the rest of the time. On a three-year-old in a Spica cast, however, they are really handy for attaching the costume to the legs. A couple of black socks, and he was a mini ninja in a stroller. You almost couldn't tell he was in a cast. That turned out to be the problem.

We set off into our idyllic suburban neighborhood to trick-or-treat. As we moved farther away from our house and our neighbors who already knew about Son Number Three's leg, a strange thing began happening. My two ambulatory sons and their cousins would run up to a door, yell "trick or treat," get their candy from the smiling suburbanite, and make their way past Number Three and me who were last in line. The once naturally smiling homeowner would then force a smile, and almost reluctantly hand over another treat to the little ninja in the stroller.

The strange looks and forced smiles continued as the evening progressed, until I paused and assessed our situation. I came around the front of the stroller to take a look at my passenger. He was in good spirits and having fun, and his costume was staying in place nicely. That's when it hit me. My wife had done too good a job of covering up the white cast with the black fabric. Standing there looking at him objectively, he looked like a perfectly normal three-year-old boy. A big, healthy three-year-old boy who should be walking, but instead was being lazily chauffeured by his ever-accommodating father. A boy at your door, lounging on two fluffy pillows, who couldn't be bothered even to sit up from his slightly reclined position to accept your free candy.

Not wanting to continue to receive what I now understood were looks of scorn, and not wanting to have to explain our situation at each door, I simply removed the sock from the fully-casted foot, and adjusted the ninja pants a little, so that people could clearly see that his foot was in a cast. That should do the trick.

Holy cow, what a difference. We went from, "Taking it easy tonight, huh?" to "Oh, bless his little heart! Here, have five pieces of candy and a balloon." It was a whole different world.

Things started to go downhill, morally speaking, from there. I have never been one to play the sympathy card, but the sheer increase in candy output we were seeing from the little bit of cast showing was astounding. Then the Reese's Peanut Butter Cups started showing up, and I lost all sense of decency. I love Reese's Peanut Butter Cups, and the freer they are, the better they taste.

I don't want to relive my downward spiral of shame and peanut buttery goodness in too great a detail, so let's suffice it to say that by the end of the night I had the entire cast on display, a three-year-old who was trained to say, "It just hurts so much," whenever I said the code phrase, "little trooper," a stroller underside cargo basket loaded down with forty-five pounds of candy, and no dignity left whatsoever.

Was it worth it? Were the endless peanut butter cups worth the price of my soul?

Absolutely! Dignity is overrated, but Reese's can't be beat.

All I can hope for is that Son Number Three is too young to remember the lesson he was taught by his unscrupulous reprobate of a dad. Now, if you will excuse me, I need to go buy his older brothers' silence with some more of my Kit Kat bars and grab another peanut butter cup from my stash. Man, those things are good!

The Spica Cast, Part IV
December 7, 2011

Son Number Three was freed from his personal fiberglass prison on the day before Thanksgiving. It was a very liberating day for all of us. He was cut loose from his huge Spica body cast, and after an entire box of baby wipes and two baths, we were finally free of his tremendously powerful ammonia smell.

While we are thrilled to finally be free of the stench, we have been left with another rather unpleasant side effect: Diapers. It's our own fault really. We all got lazy.

At the time he broke his leg, our three-year-old was potty trained, but semi-unreliable. He was wearing big boy underwear during the days, and he always alerted us to when he needed to visit the potty, but his bodily function recognition system was still being debugged. He would announce that he needed to go pee, and then proceed to poop. He would say that he needed to poop, then get to the toilet, pee, and tell us, "There is no poop in my butt." To complicate things, he also got it right half the time, so you couldn't just go with the opposite and be confident. Needless to say, after a few mix-ups while standing in front of the potty, he was a permanent sitter.

When he came home from the hospital in the crazy immobilizing uni-cast, he was no longer able to sit on the potty. To compensate for that, the hospital sent him home with a plastic wide-mouth bottle for peeing, and a plastic bed pan for pooping. Neither one was universal, and it was very difficult to get him positioned to try and use both the bottle and the bed pan at once. Given his lack of reliability on identifying what might be leaving his body at any given moment, you can see our dilemma. It was like a very high stakes game of whack-a-mole. You'd best be quick.

122

Once the cast went on, he was in diapers anyway, because the last thing you want with a Spica cast is an accident that you can't get rid of for six and a half weeks. We tried our best to use the bed pan and pee bottle for the first few days, but then we got lazy and tired of trying our best. And tired of cleaning pee out of the carpet. And out of our shirts.

By the end of Son Number Three's first week in the cast, we were having this conversation:
"I have to pee."
"OK. Go for it."
"Are you coming?"
"No, buddy. Just pee in your diaper. I'll change you right after you're done so you won't have a wet diaper."
"OK."

By the end of the second week, he was getting lazy and no longer giving us advanced notice, and we were all getting more comfortable with wet diapers:
"I peed in my diaper."
"OK, buddy."
"Are you coming?"
"Not right now. I'll change you after your show is over."
"OK."

By the end of the third week, a total family laziness had set in and we were getting no notices at all:
"Hey, buddy, it's dinner time. Do you have a wet diaper?"
"No."
"Let's check anyway… Holy cow, dude. This diaper is full."
"Oh, yeah. I peed."
"When did you pee?"
"At lunch."

So now, here we are, two weeks after he was liberated from Spica cast confinement, and he is still in diapers and still not giving us any notice. We seem to be back at square one, potty training-wise, and it looks like we're going to have to go through the whole ordeal again. We haven't started yet, though.

Why, you ask? Well, there's another problem. He hasn't started to walk yet, either.

I contend it has to do with an overall laziness that has taken over every aspect of his life, but my wife keeps telling me it's all part of the healing process. She also keeps pointing out how readily and vigorously he scoots himself around the house on his butt. She has a point. He does scoot an awful lot in situations where walking would be easier. I still think he's milking it a little, but in any case, the point is, he hasn't started back to walking yet.

What does that have to do with re-potty training, you ask? Let me give you a visual to help answer that question.

Imagine a three-year-old boy, who can't walk because of a bad leg, who wants to sit in a chair. How does he do it? Well, first, he scoots on his butt over to the chair, straddling the chair with his legs. Then he hugs the leg of the chair, putting his face on the top part of the chair leg to gain some amount of leverage. He then proceeds to use his arms and face to grapple and shimmy his way up the leg of the chair, using his good leg to push and slide head-first onto the seat, until his belly is square in the middle of the chair. He then performs a complicated flip-scoot-twist-and-sit maneuver to get into an upright sitting position on the chair.

Now imagine that with a toilet.

We're going to go ahead and just roll with the diapers a little longer until he starts to walk again.

124

7

Sports

The true test of a man's will to live is his son's soccer season.

A Hearty Soccer Dad
October 20, 2010

My wife is very sneaky. Either that, or I don't listen. I prefer to think of her as sneaky, but it's probably the latter. Either way, due to her sneakiness or my inability to pay attention, this past spring I ended up being a baseball coach without my prior knowledge. I showed up to my oldest son's first T-ball practice ready to watch from the bleachers, and she handed me a jersey and a hat and said, "By the way, you're coaching."

"What!?! Honey, I have no idea what the schedule looks like! I don't have a clue if I can make any of the practices or the games!"
"Don't worry, you can make all of them."
"Oh, OK... Well kids, who wants to try to hit my curve ball?"
"It's T-ball, honey."
"OK. Who wants to make dirt circles with their cleats?"

So, toward the end of this summer when my wife casually mentioned that our oldest would be starting soccer this year, I immediately got defensive.

"Honey, I don't know the first thing about soccer! It's been thirty-two years since I played AYSO, and I was a goalie, because I didn't understand it then, either. There is no way I can…"

"Relax, Captain Overreaction, you're not the coach."

"OK, great. When's the first game?"

After experiencing coaching kindergarteners first-hand, I was looking forward to a relaxing soccer season, sitting on the sidelines in my lawn chair, leading my two youngest boys in "Ra-Ra-Sis-Boom-Ba" cheers as we watched their older brother dominate the field and score goal after exciting goal.

That didn't happen.

I arrived with my family at the soccer fields the first Saturday morning completely unprepared for what I would experience. Not unprepared in a "did we forget something?" sense, because believe me, we didn't. The soccer game was only scheduled to last one hour, but I was packing more gear than I would normally take camping for a week. Chairs, blankets, water bottles, snacks, beach umbrellas, shade tents, hats, jackets, coolers… we almost didn't fit in the Ford Expedition.

I had inquired a couple of times to my wife that morning as to why we needed so much stuff, to which she finally responded, "Shut up and help me close this tailgate."

I started to get a feel for the program when we turned down the street toward the soccer fields. I remember the soccer fields of my youth looking something like this: Grass fields with goals on each end with kids playing soccer and parents standing on the sidelines watching. I saw none of that at first. What I saw looked like a cross between an upscale refugee camp and the midway at a state fair. Shade tents were everywhere, but it was only 78 degrees. There were four soccer fields laid out side by side, and the areas in between them were so full of chairs, blankets, umbrellas, shade tents and coolers that it was hard to discern which field they were set up to view.

Twenty minutes later, after I had unloaded the car, we began to make our way past the ends of the fields, looking for the field that my son would soon dominate. At the first field I noticed that each team had a four by eight-foot vinyl banner, staked into the ground on their respective sidelines, being held in place with very well-made PVC banner stands. The banners weren't homemade. They were the real deal, straight out of the custom print shop. Any U.S. corporation would be proud to have banners that nice at their next trade show. They were professionally printed, emblazoned with the team names and artistic logos. One had a flaming soccer ball and the other had an alligator wearing soccer cleats. They both had all the players' names on them, ensuring only one season of useful life.

"What couple of over-achiever parents came up with those?" I wondered aloud.
"Every team has one, including ours. You helped pay for it."
"I did what?... This is the five and six-year-old league, right?"
"Get over it, sweetheart."

We reached our field, and the other team dads and I spent the next twenty minutes setting up our tent city. By the time we finished, it was game time. Time for my son to dominate the soccer field!

I have already mentioned that I was unprepared for this new experience. This was not due to the game being more thrilling than I had anticipated. My son didn't dominate anything. No child on the field dominated anything. The hopeful feelings I had about an exciting and action-packed soccer match quickly vanished with the first play near the goal.

We had the ball.
One of our boys kicked the ball toward the opposing goal.
The parents leaned forward in their seats.

127

He stood and admired his kick.

The other players stood and admired his kick.

The ball rolled in front of the goal.

The goalie, not two feet from the ball, stood and admired his kick.

Some of our players and some of their players ran toward the ball.

The parents leapt to their feet in anticipation of a happening of some kind.

The two teams' players arrived at the ball at the same time.

They stopped.

No one was sure whose turn it was to kick it.

They discussed it.

The parents lurched forward, hearts in their throats, shouting, "Kick it!"

No one kicked it.

The goalie wandered over and picked it up.

The parents fell back into their seats, hands thrown into the air, looking at each other with desperate and wild eyes.

"Why didn't they kick it?"

We repeated that process no less than forty times over the course of the first half.

There is the emotion and thrill of a fast-paced professional sporting event, and then there is the raw, gut-wrenching, breath-taking angst that comes from a sporting event where nothing is happening like it should. The sheer amount of highs and lows we experienced inside a five-minute period was enough to leave a healthy adult gasping for air. My head pounded. My heart palpitated. My palms sweated. I was emotionally and physically drained. And absolutely nothing had happened.

When the other team finally scored a goal against us in the third quarter, it was strangely welcome. They had scored against us, which was not the situation I was rooting for, but at the same time, I was so darned relieved that an actual play had occurred with an actual outcome, I found myself happy and momentarily at peace. When the post-goal wave of normalcy rolled over me, I realized for the first time that day just how tense the game was making me.

I'm not sure what it is about soccer. I mean, nothing worked quite right when I coached these same aged boys and girls in T-ball, but it wasn't nearly as nerve-wracking to watch. It probably has to do with the fact that the soccer ball is always in play, so we the parents are always expecting the players to actually keep playing. When they stop with the ball at center field to inspect the grass or chase a butterfly, it is tolerable, and even humorous to witness. But when the ball is mere inches from the goal and all the players seem to suddenly forget what to do next, the breathless anticipation is almost too much to bear.

Whatever the reason, I was watching five and six-year-olds play soccer, and the emotional strain was so great, I was actually starting to worry about a possible sideline heart attack. I'm almost forty now. I have to start taking my heart health seriously!

So, after the game, the team dads got together and we decided to all chip in and buy one of those portable defibrillators. The way we figure it, if the kids don't improve to a level of at least kicking the ball and following it, the chances are pretty good that one of us is going down before the season is over.

It was an expensive unit, but we figured, what the heck, we already bought an expensive banner, and there's no way that thing is going to save one of our lives. I guess when we finally revive the first poor, unfortunate dad who succumbs to the cardiac arrest-inducing inaction on the field, we can always break down the PVC stand and use the banner as a stretcher.

The Event Planning Calendar
February 9, 2011

My mother-in-law recently threw a party for her father – my wife's grandpa – for his ninety-third birthday. Between friends and family, more than sixty people were invited to what was surely one of the biggest and most important family events of the year. She threw this party on Saturday, February 5th.

In late January I had been wandering through our kitchen and happened to peruse the calendar for upcoming events. When I noticed that we were scheduled to be at my wife's folk's house on Saturday the 5th, I immediately questioned my wife.

"Why does this say we will be in Morro Bay next weekend?"
"It's my grandpa's birthday party on Saturday."
"Excuse me?"
"IT'S MY GRANDPA'S BIRTHDAY PARTY!" (Sometimes she mistakes my incredulous voice for me being hard of hearing.)
"I heard you the first time. I just don't believe it."
"Why?"
"Why?!? The 6th is Superbowl Sunday!"
"Oh."

Oh? That's all I get? I couldn't believe it. The birthday party was being held three hundred and seventeen miles away from our house. It takes us five hours to get there if there is no traffic and no pee breaks. This is California, so there is always traffic, and we have three kids, so instead of no pee breaks, we have about thirty pee breaks every hundred miles. (To be fair to the kids, more than a few of the pee breaks are instigated by their soda-drinking parents.)

I stared at my wife, and she just stared right back. It was obvious I would get no help from her in rectifying this mess.

130

I called my mother-in-law.

"Is your dad's birthday party really on the 5th?
"Yes, why?"
"Because the 6th is the Superbowl!"
"Oh, whoops."

Whoops?!? Again, not the satisfying solution to the problem that I was looking for. I realize that she had more logistics to worry about than just my schedule, but come on. Who throws a party for out-of-town guests on Superbowl weekend? It became clear to me that I would be waking up on Superbowl Sunday six to seven hours away from my television. I had already invited people over to our house to watch the game. I could cancel that plan and stay in Morro Bay to watch the game with my wife's family, which would be fun, but I would have to take a day off work to do it. I like to use my sick days for when I'm really sick, or when there is a meeting I need to avoid, so I didn't want to burn one on this.

This event scheduling debacle really highlighted for me the need for a universal nationwide calendar of blackout dates for party and event planners. I mean, come on, ladies! The Superbowl is only the single-largest and most watched sporting event of the year. I would have thought you might have heard it was coming up.

We obviously need: The Universal Event Planning Calendar of No-Go Dates Due to Sporting Events and Other Guy Stuff.

The calendar would include the obvious sports that every American party planner should already be aware of; namely, NFL and college football, NBA and college basketball, major league baseball, golf, hockey, and Nascar. It would also include the lesser-known but still relevant sports, such as the Olympics (both summer and winter), pro rodeo, soccer, minor league baseball, Indy cars, tennis, curling, rugby, logging competitions, boxing, Scottish highland games, lacrosse, and the Tour de France.

We will need to include hunting and fishing seasons on the calendar as well. Nothing spoils a wedding faster than an absent groom who's off in a duck blind because his fiancé forgot to check the calendar. Seasons that should be included are deer, elk, moose, duck, pheasant, salmon, and steelhead. Again, the calendar will need to include the slightly lesser-known, but equally important seasons for dove, quail, snipe, ground squirrel, mockingbird, catfish, opossum, mongoose, tree squirrel, and tiger shark.

In addition to the obvious sports and hunting categories listed above, the calendar will also need to include major non-sporting events. Whether us guys choose to attend personally, or catch all the action on TV, these events cannot be missed. They include Octoberfest, all three of the triple crown horse races, any major WWF, WWE or MMA fight, the world series of poker, and the running of the bulls. A few lesser-known events will, again, need to be included if this calendar is to be deemed at all credible. These include Novemberfest, the all-Mexico bull fighting series, the inter-Irish pub darts championships, Septemberfest, the world series of canasta, and Decemberfest.

Basically, if you want to throw a party or have a wedding, you need to do it on Saturday, July 23rd. That's our only open date.

If the birthday party had been on July 23rd, I wouldn't have had to haul my kids out of bed at 3:30 in the morning to be home in time for the pregame show! Could someone get started putting that calendar together?

Fun-raising
March 2, 2011

My oldest son is in kindergarten, and two out of our three boys are playing T-ball this year, so I have begun a new chapter in my life. I now shake people down for money. The different organizations usually call it "fundraising," but let's be serious about what we're doing. Extortion. Coercion. Racketeering. That's more like it.

When you need to demand cash from people in the name of children's sports and education, there are three main target groups, the first of which is your family. The grandparents are easy money. They're good for whatever you're selling. We don't even ask anymore, we just put them down for ten of whatever it is. Now, when they call, they just ask how much they owe us this month.

Your brothers and sisters are a little harder to convince, however, since they are likely in the middle of their own fundraising activities and were just about to call *you*. In the end, you just trade money. The extended family is hit and miss, because a lot of them have stopped answering the phone.

Your next target group is your co-workers. This is where the term, "I gave at the office," comes from. As with many events in your youth, you don't really understand the circle of life moments you're living until you are completing the circle many years later. When I was in my twenties and my bosses and older coworkers came to me with the Scholastic book fair order form, or the Girl Scout cookies, I always made sure to buy as much as I could after doing some quick math in my head to make sure I would have enough money left for beer. The reason I obliged their request was purely political, however. When your boss comes to you selling something for his cute little daughter, you say, "Yes."

What I didn't understand was that I was just prepaying to cover my turn, ten to twenty years down the road. School and sports fundraising at the office is really just a giant book/cookie/raffle ticket/magazine pyramid scheme. I bought your ticket into the club, now it's your turn to buy mine.

The third target group is the neighbors. This market lets you use a different and very persuasive technique: Taking the kids with you. Who could say no to the cute little five-year-old with the big blue eyes explaining all about how they need to raise money to fulfill their lifelong dream of hitting a ball with a bat? Anyone who answers the door is toast. The problem is, they have the option of pretending they're not home. Make no mistake about it, when they see you coming with the kids, holding an order form, they know what's about to go down.

"Daddy, didn't we just see him come home? How come he's not answering the door?"
"He must be in the shower, son. Let's go. I'll have a little chat with Bob later."
"How come the curtains are moving?"
"Probably the cat. Let's go to the next house, son. WE'LL COME BACK TOMORROW AT DINNER TIME SO WE'LL BE SURE TO AVOID MISSING BOB AGAIN!"
"How come you're talking so loud, Dad?"
"Never mind."

Going door to door in the neighborhood is a fun and enlightening experience. My sons have no idea how valuable an education in human behavior they are receiving simply by standing on someone else's front porch, asking for money. There are three types of neighborhood buyers: The people who are buying your five-dollar raffle ticket because you brought the kids with you and they don't want to say no; the ones who are thrilled about the opportunity to help out and happily purchase a ticket; and the ones like me, who have simply resigned themselves to the fact that this is just part of having kids. We don't bat an eye, we just hand over the cash.

If I didn't need to take the boys with me as a sales tool and for their own education, I would approach it completely differently.

"Look, Bob, here's the deal. I need to sell twenty of these raffle tickets. You're only on the hook for one. You won't win the big screen TV, or the five hundred-dollar gift card, so let's not kid ourselves. We both know the odds. Just give me the five bucks you were going to spend on your latte tomorrow morning and I promise to buy whatever the hell your kid is going to be selling next week, OK? You and I both know your waistline could use a few less lattes anyway, partner. You're welcome."

It would really be a lot simpler if we just self-funded these things, but what would that teach the kids?

The Hydration of a Thirsty Nation
March 9, 2011

"Why is everyone so thirsty all of a sudden?" That's what my grandpa used to ask me. "Nowadays everyone carries around their own personal bottle of water. They all must be really thirsty." He was amazed and amused by the sight of it.

Nation-wide thirst has, indeed, increased dramatically in my lifetime. Think back to when you were a kid. Do you remember anyone ever walking around holding their own personal bottle of water? No. Because personal water bottles didn't exist. Somewhere along the line – in the late 1980s, I think – companies first produced the portable plastic personal bottle of water, and we have been a nation on the verge of dehydration ever since.

The invention of the personal bottle of water was huge - bigger than the cell phone, probably - because it spans all the generation gaps. Every single man, woman, and child needs their own bottle of water today. Everyone from the eighty-year-olds to the one-year-olds can be seen fighting off imminent dehydration with their very own 0.75-liter Evian life insurance policy. This was a massive double-play for beverage companies, because not only does the target market consist of everyone, but they had finally figured out how to get people to pay for something that was otherwise free. That really made my grandpa laugh.

I began to realize how truly water-crazy we have become when my kids started playing organized sports. Every kid on my son's soccer team arrived at the first practice with their own water bottle. Some kids had those Thermos-type one-gallon jugs with the flip-top spout. They played soccer for about three minutes and then had a ten-minute water break. When I was a kid playing soccer we practiced for an hour and then you were more than welcome to go find a drinking fountain somewhere if you were thirsty. On game days, the parents brought orange slices. You weren't allowed to leave the field to find a drinking fountain, so you got any liquid you might need from the orange pulp.

With my son's team, they cancelled a few of the practices because it was too hot. I was left thinking, "Are they actually worried anyone will overheat? Between all the players and coaches they will have four hundred gallons of water within arm's reach. They could take what they don't drink and fill a small swimming pool if they get too hot." Oh, well.

And, don't even get me started on T-ball. If there was ever a sport that requires as little movement as possible on the player's part, it's T-ball. I have never seen any of the players actually break a sweat, yet our entire squad comes equipped with giant personal tankards of liquids. We are constantly rotating kids off the field in the middle of games to go pee, and the floor of our dugout is like a spring water minefield.

And not content with just plain old water anymore, many parents opt for sports drinks to keep their kid's electrolyte levels acceptable. I know the electrolyte levels of us kids was always a big concern for my folks.

The shift in our perceived water requirements is a strange thing. Back in the day, if you were ever thirsty when you were outside playing, you found a drinking fountain or a hose. Nowadays, moms and dads actually follow their children around the playgrounds and parks with bottles of water, forcing them to drink water even if the kids protest that they're not thirsty. On any given 70-degree day you'll hear, "You have to drink some water, Billy. It's hot out here!" Many of today's moms may not believe this, but farmers used to work all day in the fields, only drinking water at meal times. Many of today's moms also may not believe that pee is supposed to be yellow, not clear.

I used to work with a guy who was a coffee drinker and a smoker. He had been with the company for years running one of the machines out in the shop. One day I wandered over to his workstation holding a cup of water. He asked me what I was drinking, and when I told him, he said, "Hmm. I can't remember the last time I had a drink of water." He was dead serious. He thought about it for a while and decided that he hadn't had so much as a sip of plain old water in over ten years. Wrap your head around that one, Mommy!

My wife is one of "today's moms" who feels the need to keep herself and our three boys maximally hydrated. I am starting to think an over-abundance of water in the body sort of feeds on itself like a crack addiction, because no matter how much water we give him, Son Number Two is constantly complaining about being thirsty. He is also the one that needs to go to the bathroom every eight minutes. Strangely enough, he is also the one who has had the most potty training issues and nighttime "accidents."

It occurs to me that our potty training might go a little smoother if our boys weren't experiencing a level-nine bladder emergency every time they need to pee. In fact, I'm not sure that any of them have ever had just a simple urge to pee. It's always been a zero-to-sixty rush to the toilet to unleash a fire hose.

They say the human body is about sixty percent water. I'd ask them to re-check. I'll bet these days we're more like eighty percent. And I'll bet my boys are pushing ninety-five.

There goes one of them now, sprinting to the bathroom.

Better Living through Mediocrity
June 1, 2011

This was my second year as an assistant T-ball coach, and this year we had two of our three boys playing. Thankfully, they were on the same team. Our regular-season activities ended last Saturday, and would have ended a full week earlier had we not been making up some early-season rain-outs. It was a pretty busy year for us, sports-wise, but I'm almost positive that every year from now on will be busier. Next year, all three boys will play, and they will all be on different teams. The parental logistics of that will be interesting, to say the least.

This year, we had four players on our T-ball team that stood out head and shoulders above the rest in terms of skill. Thankfully, I was not related to any of them. My boys were mediocre, and that's just how we like them. Allow me to explain.

The four best players from our team were recruited toward the end of the season to play on championship teams. (Keep in mind that these are five and six-year-olds. We take our baseball pretty seriously here in Rocklin.) Those four kids were going to extra practices during the tail end of our season, and they all played in a Memorial Day weekend tournament.

Now, you may hear "Memorial Day weekend tournament," and think, "Sounds like fun." We went to watch a few of the games, and while there were many fun and exciting moments, the tournament was also very time-consuming. Not for my family, mind you, but for the families of the all-stars.

My family and I were free to do whatever we wanted over the long weekend. We ended up at the ballpark to watch a few games, but we also slept late in the mornings, made two trips to friends' houses for dinners, and generally set our own schedule. The families of the all-stars were not so lucky. The tournament

139

ruled their schedules. When asked what they had planned for the long weekend, they were forced to answer, "I don't know. It depends on how we do in the tournament."

These scheduling woes didn't apply to just the baseball families, either. On Sunday afternoon, we stopped by a local college campus to meet one of my wife's good friends. Her daughter was playing in a youth soccer tournament, and her whole family had been there, an hour's drive from their home, for two full days. I asked her how her daughter was doing in the tournament, and in an antithetically dejected voice she replied, "They keep winning. We were supposed to be at a friend's house for dinner, but we have to stay for the championship game. The other two kids are bummed out because they wanted to see their friends, but instead, we all need to stay here."

Long weekends aside, kids' sports can also affect vacation plans. About a week ago, our good friends from college had to send us regrets and cancel their plans to come up from Southern California to go to Lake Tahoe for a week. We were planning on meeting up with them there at the end of June, but their oldest son ended up being one of twelve eight-year-olds picked out of one hundred thirty to be in an all-star baseball tournament.

Witnessing this all-star ball-and-chain effect that so many of our friends are going through got me thinking. Kids' hopes and dreams are one thing, but what about mine? I have hopes and dreams, too. One of them is to be able to sit down every once in a while, and not have every Saturday for the rest of my life already booked with one of my kid's sporting events. I am the father of what appear to be three rather promising-looking boys in the sports and athletics department. So far, they are a little too young to be shining, but I fear that it is only a matter of time.

Back when they were born and I was a proud and naïve papa, I was no doubt looking forward to them holding the trophy high

140

above their heads one day. Now, the more I see, the more I think mediocrity might be the ticket.

"Maybe we don't need to practice so much in the backyard, Son. Why don't you go burn leaves and ants with a magnifying glass instead?"

Don't get me wrong. I still want them to play sports, just not in an outstanding manner that may cause the seasons to be extended in any way. My new plan is to shoot for third place. That way, I might actually get to go fishing every once in a while.

"What are you doing this summer, Bob?"
"We're committed through August with Junior's baseball Champions Bracket. How about you, Smidge?"
"Not us! Did you see my kid drop that grounder at shortstop during the last game? No way he was going to make the post-season. We're going to Cabo!"

"Hey, Smidge. Did you hear about the baseball clinic that the college baseball coach is putting on for the kids? Only a hundred and thirty bucks for three days!"
"Not interested, Phil. My boys aren't big league material. No sense fighting facts."

"Hey Smidge, want to enroll your kids in Taekwondo?"
"What are they going to be, the next Jackie Chan? No, thanks. I'd like to keep at least some of my money, and maybe a few of my evenings and weekends free."

"Want to enroll your kids in our two-week soccer camp?"
"No, thanks. The regular soccer season is painful enough. And let's face it, soccer as a professional sport is never going to catch on in America, so I don't really see the point in the first place."

I think I am going to extend my third place approach into their academics as well. Based on the size of their heads, their mom's DNA, and their incredible Lego skills, my kids will probably end up being pretty smart. That being said, I plan to encourage and nurture their education only to the point that it does not interfere with my life.

They will be required to maintain good grades, but will be expressly forbidden from joining any sort of academic club that has extra-curricular activities. The last thing I want is to have successfully thwarted post-season athletics and accidentally end up stuck at a chess tournament or a debate club's weekend rebuttal-o-rama.

The problem is, holding them back might end up being more difficult than I think. We may be able to keep them at bay with enough TV, but it's going to be touch-and-go. Son Number One is proving to be a pretty good piano player, Number Two is quite a little over-achiever, both academically and physically, and Number Three is already a wicked switch hitter at three years old. It's not looking good.

If you'll excuse me now, I have to go hide the bats and balls and turn on the TV. Forget your homework, boys, let's watch some Disney channel!

Soccer as Birth Control
August 31, 2011

As an example of how crazy we have become, I will start with communications. When I played soccer as a youth, I am quite certain that my parents probably saw one flyer at the beginning of the year, outlining the practice schedule. There was probably a one-page flyer handed out at the first or second practice that outlined the game schedule for the entire season, and that was that. With two pieces of paper, everyone knew where they needed to be and when.

When it was time for soccer practice, I was told to get on my bike and go to soccer practice. Why on Earth would my parents have driven me there, let alone stayed for the entire practice to watch? That was what the coach was for. When practice was over, the coach told us to go home. Simple.

Fast-forward to today. As I write this, I am sitting in a lawn chair watching Son Number Two's soccer practice. The miracle of modern tablet computers makes this possible, but does not answer the question of, "Why am I here?"

When did a child's sports practice become so important to us that we now feel the need to have it take up an hour-plus of the parent's time also? I don't have the exact answer for that, but I do know it happened sometime in between when I was a kid and when I had kids of my own.

There has been an obvious shift in how safe we feel the world is, because parents today don't let their kids travel across town by themselves as readily as our parents did. As a result, we are raising a generation of kids who get lost a block from their own houses, but that's a separate subject. The safety issue explains why the parents drive their kids to practice, but not necessarily why they stay to watch. I guess a lot of it has to do with

143

excessive trips. Once I'm here, I might as well just hang around until it's over. The occasional parent runs a quick errand, but for the most part, they just pull up a lawn chair and worry about their child dehydrating, or marvel at why two grown men can't get nine five-years-olds to stand still in a straight line even if their lives depended on it.

Now, back to the communication issue. In stark contrast to the two paper flyers that handled the logistics for an entire soccer season of my youth, today's soccer leagues run on e-mails. A lot of e-mails. Based on my experiences so far, to run a youth soccer team these days requires approximately three e-mails per day be sent to each parent, starting two months before the first practice and never missing a day throughout the whole season.

There are vital logistical issues to address on an almost hourly basis, such as team banner design and procurement, uniform sizes, proper cleat specifications for the particular league, the heat index, the air quality index, proper child hydration techniques, acceptable soccer ball sizes, fluctuating practice schedules, fluctuating practice locations, raffle ticket distribution and sales, team sponsor procurement, team parent selection, game day halftime snack coordination, team sponsor patronage, game day post-game treat coordination, game day halftime snack and post-game treat food allergy considerations, coach and team parent fingerprinting and FBI background check verification, elementary school extracurricular activity scheduling conflicts, end-of-year party location and party theme, individual end-of-year trophy selection and procurement, game day sideline bench procurement or manufacture, game day sideline bench assembly duty schedule, opening day ceremonies schedule, sideline shade tent ownership queries, game day sideline shade tent assembly duties, coach and team parent end-of-season gift coordination, proper shin guard selection and management, picture and video collection for end-of-season media DVD, game day jersey color, etcetera, etcetera.

144

I have no good reason for why the amount of perceived soccer team management logistical hurdles has increased exponentially since my youth. Is it because now that we all have e-mail at our fingertips every minute of the day, we can finally take care of *everything* that **needs** to happen? Would all of these issues have been addressed in earnest if our parents hadn't been severely hampered by a lack of technology?

Somehow, I doubt it.

Like I said, I don't know why soccer has become so complex, but I am convinced that its newfound complexity is having a major impact on our society. Specifically regarding how many children we have. I truly believe as new families are growing, and young parents are considering adding a new bundle of joy to the lineup, the logistics of having those kids eventually play soccer has more of a role in the decision making process than almost anything else in the mix today.

"Honey, I realize that we always wanted a girl, but with two boys already in soccer, how can we even think about a third child? We don't even have enough time to keep up with the practices and e-mails with the two kids we already have."

8

Getting Older

It happens to everyone, but that still doesn't make it OK.

Ten-Year Warranty
February 23, 2011

Ten years isn't as long as it used to be. When I was a kid, ten years was a lifetime. That's probably because when you're ten years old, ten years is literally a lifetime. When you get to twenty, ten years still seems like a pretty long time, and thirty seems really old. When you finally get to thirty, you don't feel old at all, and you are starting to have an appreciation for how much time seems to be speeding up, but forty still seems like a long way off. Well, I'm almost forty now, and I can assure those of you who are still in your twenties, I only turned thirty about six months ago. At least, it sure seems that way.

A lot has happened since I turned thirty. I got married and had three kids, for starters. I was a carefree youngster ten years ago. Now I'm a really responsible guy known around the house as, "Daddy." Our oldest son is six, but that's impossible, because there is no way I've been a dad for over six years. We only had him a couple of years ago, max. At least, it sure seems that way.

The passage of time has a way of accelerating as you grow older, and apparently it really kicks into high gear around age forty.

146

I noticed the other day that almost everything we bought or received right around the time we got married seems to be falling apart. The waffle maker is shooting craps, the gift-registry china is all chipped, the blender leaks, the ridiculously expensive duvet cover (that's fancy-talk for blanket) is showing signs of wear, and don't even get me started on the bed itself. Our California king now has two deep sleep-valleys on either side and a large mountain range that resides directly between us. If I want to visit my wife on her side of the bed, I have to get climbing gear and mount an expedition over the king-sized continental divide.

As I'm noticing all these heavily used items recently, I keep thinking, "This thing can't possibly be worn out yet! We've only had it for a year or two." That's the problem with this time acceleration phenomenon we all face. If I stop and think about when we got the item in question, I realize it's almost a decade old. But it still tends to be really aggravating, because it doesn't seem at all possible that it could have been that long.

However, the *things* in the house wearing out are, unfortunately, not the biggest concern I'm facing right now. It's the *who* in the house that is wearing out that has me really worried. Namely, me. I, myself, happen to be deteriorating at an alarming rate, and that is much more concerning to me than what has happened to the duvet cover.

When I was twenty I was damn-near bullet-proof. I could see like an eagle and run like a cheetah. My hair looked cool, my waist was slim, and my muscles were like steel springs. If I broke my leg at 4:00 P.M. it would be healed by 8:00 the next morning, and I bounced out of bed every day ready to tackle the world. I was poor and stupid, but I was quick and tough.

When I was thirty, not much had changed from that. I wasn't quite as poor, and I was a whole lot smarter, but I was still virtually bullet-proof. Actually, I was probably only bullet-resistant at that point, but I still felt great every day.

Now, not even a full ten years later, I am a train wreck. My belly has become quite a bit fatter, while my butt seems to be disappearing. The vast majority of the hair on my head has left for good, and much of it seems to have migrated onto my neck and upper back. I have intermittent neck pain that can be temporarily relieved by cracking the vertebrae in my neck so loudly that it makes my wife jump. I've got a calcium deposit on one of my elbows that you could chalk like a pool cue, and my knees hurt when I go up and down stairs. I have a form of arthritis in one of my big toes that prevents it from bending backward properly, and my podiatrist tells me it will require surgery to fix. My good cholesterol is low, my bad cholesterol is high, and if I sit on the floor for more than three minutes I will be sore for the next three days. My lower back is completely shot, and I now actually wake up more sore than when I went to bed. I can throw my back out while sleeping. One of my shoulders pops in and out when I swing my arm, and I can now only sleep on my back because my arms go totally dead when I try to sleep on my sides. My night vision has noticeably deteriorated, and my hearing is going, evidenced by the volume of the TV these days. My teeth are slowly falling apart, my brain is rapidly slowing down, my taste buds are dulling, and I have developed some really wicked seasonal allergies that if I fail to treat with prescription drugs, can make me wish for the sweet release of death.

When I turned thirty, I had an ingrown toenail. That was the full extent of my medical problems.

I'm not complaining, mind you, just marveling at how fast things can change. I know all you sixty-year-olds are laughing at me right now, saying, "Just wait, buddy. It gets worse." At this point, I just hope I make it that long to find out!

The upside is, the way time seems to be accelerating, it will only be three or four years until I'm sixty. At least, it sure seems that way.

Going Bald
July 26, 2011

I started to lose my hair about six years ago. At this point, I am at least half way to being totally bald. Apparently it is a slow process. That is probably so you will have time to adjust. (My oldest son is six and a half. I don't think that is a coincidence.)

I really miss my hair, but not why you might think. None of my reservations about going bald have anything to do with vanity. I will not miss my hair for one minute from a looks standpoint. I just never cared about it very much. If you took a look at my school pictures from K through 12, you would see that I never put much time into trying to have cool hair.

It appears that there was a brief period in the eighties when I actually tried to have a hair style, but unfortunately, like so many other things in the eighties, it was ill-advised. Apparently – and fortunately – it lasted less than a year, because it is captured for posterity in only one of my school pictures. Seventh grade will forever be known as the year of the part down the middle with super-cool feathered bangs. This was the same year that I had braces with headgear, so looking back on it, I was probably trying desperately to compensate for having a stainless steel wire sticking out of my mouth, attached by rubber bands to a "flesh colored" (read: pink) neck strap. That would also explain the rolled up cuffs on my jeans with the black-and-white checkered slip-on Vans with no socks. Trust me, at the time, that seemed to be the height of fashion. But like I said, it was the eighties. Bad choices all the way around.

I either got rid of the headgear, or just got tired of paying attention to my hair, because by the eighth grade photo I was back to short hair. I have kept it short ever since. Up until I went bald, I had never viewed my hair as an asset. I never really thought of it as a liability, either. I think I just never thought

150

much about it at all. It has always been just a line-item on a to-do list. Morning: wash hair. Every two weeks: cut hair. In that regard, my hair is a lot like the front lawn. I don't give either one much thought; I just water and cut them both on a regular schedule. Like the front lawn, I don't mind cutting my hair, but past that, I want no other maintenance activities taking up even an extra minute of my time.

So, given that I put my hair in the same category as lawn maintenance, you may be asking yourself, why would he miss it? Seems like it would be a good thing not to have to deal with it anymore. I agree. I was actually pretty excited about the less-maintenance aspect of my hair loss. Until I went outside…

I'm not sure you can fully appreciate this unless you yourself have actually gone bald, but the hair on top of your head is an amazing source of insulation. When I go outside now in the slightest whisper of cold air, I am instantly freezing. If the sun is out and it's over 65 degrees, I'm burning up. For the first time in my life, I am a wuss. I need a hat at all times.

I was blown away by what a difference having no hair makes on my body temperature. Apparently, it doesn't take very much hair to keep you insulated, either, since my hair was never over a half-inch long. I guess as long as it's evenly distributed, length really doesn't count for too much.

This constant need for a hat has thrown me for a loop. It has introduced a whole new level of planning into my formerly simple life. I used to just go places. Time to go? Let's see… I'm wearing clothes… OK, I'm ready! Now, when it's time to go, I have to make decisions. Where are we going? What are we doing? Is it an indoor event? Is there even the remotest possibility that we will be outside, even for a few minutes? Not sure? Better bring a hat just in case.

Now I am forced to find a hat that will "go" with my clothes, or my wife won't stand next to me. I am forced to choose from a selection of baseball-type caps, since I am not anywhere cool enough to be able to pull off the fedora or the Kangol driver's cap look, and my cowboy hat always seems a bit much for a backyard barbeque. In hot weather, I always really want to wear one of my wide-brimmed, floppy, "boonie" hats, but they are all some sort of camouflage pattern, so I end up looking like I am there to invade the backyard, not just visit.

You would think the baseball cap would be good enough, but let me tell you, they are not without challenges to the bald man. The adjustable size varieties have the open semi-circle in the back. I found out the hard way that I still need to apply sunscreen to the back of my head to avoid a second-degree half-moon burn. Even if the cap is fitted and does not have the dangerous rear opening, it is still not one hundred percent safe. I have had occasions when I have sat still in the sun for long enough – at a baseball game or an outdoor concert – that I have received six tiny little circular sunburns on the top of my head, through the pin-hole air vents on the top of the cap. Come on!

In the summer time, I just sunscreen my whole head on the weekends. It's just safer that way.

It is a cruel trick played on the bald man. Whether he cared about his hair when he had it or not, as soon as it's gone he is forced to accessorize. Coming from a guy who never accessorized anything, and always just had clothes instead of "outfits," this has been a pretty big adjustment for me. My wife has started to look into online tests for colorblindness, just to make sure I'm not a total idiot. (I think she's going to be sorely disappointed!)

Well, I've got to go. We've got a wedding to attend.
"Honey, which one of these ball caps goes with my suit?"

I miss my hair.

Finally Growing Up
August 10, 2011

There have been many significant events in my life that signaled to me that I was growing up. Getting my driver's license, voting for the first time, being able to legally buy beer, getting married, and buying a house all come to mind. Those were definitely milestones on the path, but the big one was, of course, having kids. Or so I thought…

Up until recently, having children of my own was the most obvious (and most pungent) signal of my inevitable maturing. There is an in-your-face responsibility that comes with having kids. They tend to get louder and louder if you're not taking care of them correctly, like an alarm clock that will not let you be late for work, no matter how many buttons you hit in an attempt to shut it off. Whatever you were planning on doing with your life before having children is suddenly a moot point. If it doesn't fit with the new directive of caring for the child, it is not in the program. I figured that surrendering to that new reality and embracing it was the final step to adulthood. Not so.

The responsibility of providing for a helpless child is a big-time kick in the pants toward becoming a full-fledged responsible adult, but it is not the final step you must take to complete the transition to one hundred percent adultness. I realized recently that there is one more step required.

Having a 401k, you ask? Hosting Thanksgiving? Buying life insurance? Writing a will?

No. The final step on the road to adulthood is not something you do, but rather, something you don't do. You have arrived at your final destination of maturity and responsibility when you are able to look at your son's Razor scooter, and not try to ride it.

When you can walk past an unattended skateboard, look at it, and say to yourself, "No thanks. I have to work tomorrow, and that's going to be more difficult with a broken arm."

When you can say that, you have arrived.

This last step towards a man's adulthood has a definite age component to it. It happens around the age of forty, give or take a few years depending on the guy and his IQ-to-pain threshold ratio. In that regard, I am lucky that I had children somewhat later in life. I am almost forty, but my oldest son is only six and a half. They don't really start owning incredibly dangerous wheeled toys until around age four or five, so I haven't had too many pre-forty years with access to lots of ulna-snapping contraptions.

I pity the guys that had kids in their twenties, because the years in between thirty and forty are the most dangerous years of a man's life. A young man in his teens and twenties will do incredibly stupid things, but this is counteracted by the fact that he has reflexes like a cheetah, and his body is made entirely out of rubber and steel. By his early thirties, the bones, ligaments and tendons have already begun to weaken and degrade, but the fear of becoming old, combined with the false ego of "not being old yet" form the perfect storm of stupidity versus degraded coordination and resilience.

Many are the thirty-eight-year-old men who have not been able to get out of bed the next day after doing nothing more than dancing at a wedding.

"I have shooting pain down my leg, my back is killing me, I can't twist my neck to the right, and don't even get me started on my rotator cuff."

"Well, honey, you did dance for over an hour."

154

When that man finally heals up from all the dancing and wakes up one day to realize that he likes being able to walk more than he likes trying to prove he can still jump the curb on a pair of Rollerblades, he has made it into the club. Some would call that growing old. I call it growing up.

Now, if you'll excuse me, I promised my son I would teach him how to do a wheelie on his bike. Don't worry, I'll be fine. I'm only thirty-nine. I'm not old yet.

* * *

ABOUT THE AUTHOR

Marc Schmatjen lives in Northern California with his wonderful wife and their three boys, two of whom are semi-normal, and one who is a total nut bar.

Marc writes adventure books for children and family humor columns for adults.

www.justasmidge.com

Made in the USA
San Bernardino, CA
21 October 2014